MW01042080

COURSE OF ACTION

Motivation, Inspiration, and Direction to Enhance Your Life

DANIEL TADDEO

PUBLISHED BY FIDELI PUBLISHING INC.

From the Author

I want to acknowledge and give deserved recognition to all known and unknown writers whose works appear in this publication. Special credit goes to Christine Wiegand, whose editing skills, attention to detail, and devotedness to this endeavor enhanced the content and message significantly.

Thank you all.

—Daniel Taddeo

Contents

Introduction

Although there are exceptions, most people agree that a universal code of ethics does exist. Any kind of order would be impossible unless all civilized people have a set of principles that determine responsible behavior. C. S. Lewis wrote, "We know that people find themselves under a moral law, which they did not make and cannot quite forget even when they try, and which they know they ought to obey."

Most agree that no society could survive without moral laws that spell out right and wrong conduct. The question then becomes: Whose morality will be legislated? All laws intrude on the morality of someone. Are there moral principles and guidelines that have withstood the unfailing test of time? I believe the answer is yes and the following pages will reveal this to the reader.

Course of Action is a unique collection of essays and "notable quotables." The focus is on two approaches to living life—Godliness vs. worldliness: sharing wisdom past and present to help individuals become the best they can be, help make families stronger, and help keep our country principled and going in a positive direction.

Godliness is determined by God's word, The Bible. Biblical principles never change; they are the same "yesterday, today and forever." The answer to America's problems does not lie in more government spending, more laws, more police, or more jails. These actions at best focus on putting out fires rather than preventing them. What the situation calls for is a return to biblical moral values on which our nation was founded.

Worldliness is determined by the secular culture. It often is the opposite of Godliness; its beliefs and prevailing conventions are constantly changing. They have been popular in the past, they remain popular in the present, and they will continue to be popular in the future. This doesn't make it right.

In our culture, we often discover too late that what we thought was right turns out to be wrong, and what we thought was wrong turns out to be right. The test for a right decision is this: Does it adhere to biblical principles?

The choice is between Godliness and worldliness. "No one can serve two masters." It's like trying to go in two different directions at the same time; you end up going in circles and you never reach your destination. Each person is responsible for deciding which path to take and what choices to make. In the end, it behooves each of us to keep in mind: "We reap what we sow." It can't be any other way!

—Daniel Taddeo

A Message to Congress

Inasmuch as our greatest leaders have shown no doubt about God's proper place in the American birthright, can we, in our day, dare do less? ...

In no other place in the United States, are there so many and such varied official evidences of deep and abiding faith in God on the part of Government as there are in Washington...

Every session of the House and Senate begins with prayer. Each house has its own chaplain.

The Eighty-third Congress set aside a small room in the Capitol, just off the rotunda, for the private prayer and meditation of members of Congress. The room is always open when Congress is in session, but it is not open to the public. The room's focal point is a stained glass window showing George Washington kneeling in prayer. Behind him is etched these words from Psalm 16:1: "Preserve us, O God, for in Thee do I put my trust."

Inside the rotunda is a picture of the Pilgrims about to embark from Holland on the sister ship of the Mayflower, the Speedwell. The ship's revered chaplain, Brewster, who later joined the Mayflower, has the Bible open on his lap. Very clear are the words, "the New Testament according to our Lord and Savior, Jesus Christ." On the sail is the motto of the Pilgrims, "In God We Trust, God With Us."

The phrase, "In God We Trust," appears opposite the President of the Senate, who is the Vice-President of the United States. The same phrase, in large words inscribed in the marble, backdrops the Speaker of the House of Representatives.

Above the head of the Chief Justice of the Supreme Court are the Ten Commandments, with the great American eagle protecting them. Moses is included among the great lawgivers in Herman A. MacNeil's marble sculpture group on the east front. The crier who opens each session closes with the words, "God save the United States and this Honorable Court."

Engraved in the metal on the top of the Washington Monument are the words: "Praise be to God." Lining the walls of the stairwell are such biblical phrases as "Search the Scriptures," "Holiness to the Lord," "Train up a child in the way he should go, and when he is old he will not depart from it."

Numerous quotations from Scripture can be found within its [the Library of Congress] walls. One reminds each American of his responsibility to his Maker: "What doth the Lord require of thee, but to **do justly** and **love mercy** and **walk humbly** with thy God." (Micah 6:8)

Another in the lawmaker's library preserves the Psalmist's acknowledgment that all nature reflects the order and beauty of the Creator: "The heavens declare the glory of God, and the firmament showeth His handiwork." (Psalm 19:1) And still another reference: "The light shineth in darkness, and the darkness comprehendeth it not." (John 1:5)

Millions have stood in the Lincoln Memorial and gazed up at the statue of the great Abraham Lincoln. The sculptor who chiseled the features of Lincoln in granite all but seems to make Lincoln speak his own words inscribed into the walls.

"...That this Nation, under God, shall have a new birth of freedom, and that government of the people, by the people, for the people, shall not perish from the earth."

At the opposite end, on the north wall, his Second Inaugural Address alludes to "God," the "Bible," "providence," "the Almighty," and "divine attributes."

It then continues: As was said 3000 years ago, so it still must be said, "The judgments of the Lord are true and righteous altogether."

On the south banks of Washington's Tidal Basin, Thomas Jefferson still speaks: "God who gave us life gave us liberty. Can the liberties of a nation be secure when we have removed a conviction that these liberties are the gift of God? Indeed I tremble for my country when I reflect that God is just, that his justice cannot sleep forever." [These words of Jefferson are] a forceful and explicit warning that to remove God from this country will destroy it.

—Senator Robert Byrd

A-Z of Life

Avoid negative sources, people, places, things, and habits.

Believe in yourself.

Consider things from every angle.

Don't give up and don't give in.

Enjoy life today; yesterday is gone; tomorrow may never come.

Family and friends are hidden treasures; seek them and enjoy their riches.

Give more than you planned to give.

Hang on to your dreams

Ignore those who try to discourage you.

Just do it.

Keep trying no matter how hard it seems; it will get easier.

Love God first and most.

Make it happen.

Never lie, cheat or steal; always strike a fair deal.

Open your eyes and see things as they really are.

Practice makes perfect.

Quitters never win and winners never quit.

Read, study and learn about everything important in your life.

Stop procrastinating.

Take control of your destiny.

Understand yourself in order to better understand others.

Visualize it.

Want it more than anything,

X-cellerate your efforts.

You are unique of all God's creations; nothing can replace you.

Zero in on your target and go for it!

—Author Unknown

An Interview with God

I dreamed I had an interview with God. "So, you would like to interview me?" God asked. "If you have the time," I said. God smiled. "My time is eternity; what questions do you have in mind to ask me?" "What surprises you most about humankind?"

God answered: "That they get bored with childhood—they rush to grow up and then long to be children again. That they lose their health to make money and then lose their money to restore their health. That by thinking anxiously about the future, they forget the present, such that they live neither the present nor the future. That they live as if they will never die, and they die as if they had never lived..."

God's hands took mine and we were silent for a while and then I asked, "As a parent, what are some of life's lessons you want your children to learn?"

God replied with a smile, "To learn that they cannot make anyone love them. What they can do is to let themselves beloved.

"To learn that what is most valuable is not what they have in their lives, but who they have in their lives.

"To learn that it is not good to compare themselves to others.

"To learn that a rich person is not the one who has the most, but is one who needs the least.

"To learn that it only takes a few seconds to open profound wounds in persons one loves, and that it may take many years to heal them.

"To learn to forgive by practicing forgiveness.

"To learn that there are persons who love them dearly, but simply do not know how to express or show their feelings.

"To learn that money can buy everything but happiness.

"To learn that two people can look at the same thing and see it very differently.

"To learn that it is not always enough that they be forgiven by others, but that they must also forgive themselves.

"And to learn that I am here—always."

—Author Unknown

Be a Blessing

Be accountable.

Be consistent.

Be dependable.

Be encouraging.

Be ethical.

Be fair.

Be friendly.

Be honest.

Be honorable.

Be humble.

Be kind.

Be merciful.

Be patient.

Be positive.

Be respectful.

Be sincere.

Be supportive.

Be sympathetic.

Be thoughtful.

Be truthful.

Bible Basics

Appearance: The Lord does not look at the things man looks at. Man looks at the outward appearance, but the Lord looks at the heart. 1 Samuel 16:7

Approach: I am the way and the truth and the life. No one comes to the Father except through me. John 14:6

Critical Times: There will be terrible times in the last days. People will be lovers of themselves, lovers of money, boastful, proud, abusive, disobedient to their parents, ungrateful, unholy, without love, unforgiving, slanderous, without self-control, brutal, not lovers of the good, treacherous, rash, conceited, lovers of pleasure rather than lovers of God—having a form of godliness but denying its power. 2 Timothy 3:1-5

Exhortations: Whatever is true, whatever is noble, whatever is right, whatever is pure, whatever is lovely, whatever is admirable— if anything is excellent or praiseworthy—think about such things. Philippians 4:8

Faith: Without faith it is impossible to please God, because anyone who comes to him must believe that he exists and that he rewards those who earnestly seek him. Hebrews 11:6

Fruit of the Spirit: The fruit of the Spirit is love, joy, peace, patience, kindness, goodness, faithfulness, gentleness and self-control. Galatians 5:22, 23

God's Word: All Scripture is God-breathed and is useful for teaching, rebuking, correcting and training in righteousness. 2 Timothy 3:16

Life: God so loved the world that he gave his one and only Son, that whoever believes in him shall not perish but have eternal life. John 3:16

Lord: What does the Lord require of you? To act justly and to love mercy and to walk humbly with your God. Micah 6:8

Mediator: There is one God and one mediator between God and men, the man Christ Jesus. 1 Timothy 2:5

Rejoice: Though the fig tree does not bud and there are no grapes on the vines, though the olive crop fails and the fields produce no food, though there are no sheep in the pen and no cattle in the stalls, yet I will rejoice in the Lord. Habakkuk 3:17, 18

Resurrection: Do not be amazed at this, for a time is coming when all who are in their graves will hear his voice and come out—those who have done good will rise to live, and those who have done evil will rise to be condemned. John 5:28, 29

Savior: I, even I, am the Lord, and apart from me there is no savior. Isaiah 43:11

Sinful Nature: The acts of the sinful nature are obvious: sexual immorality, impurity and debauchery; idolatry and witchcraft; hatred, discord, jealously, fits of rage, selfish ambition, dissensions, factions and envy; drunkenness, orgies, and the like. Galatians 5:19-21

The Greatest Commandment: Love the Lord your God with all your heart and with all your soul and with all your mind. This is the first and greatest commandment. And the second is like it: Love your neighbor as yourself. Matthew 22:37-39

Blame

Blame never affirms; it **assaults**.
Blame never restores; it **wounds**.
Blame never solves; it **complicates**.
Blame never unites; it **separates**.
Blame never smiles; it **frowns**.
Blame never forgives; it **rejects**.
Blame never builds; it **destroys**.

—John Hagee

The blame game is as old as the Garden of Eden. Can't you just see Adam and Eve pointing fingers at each other and at that grinning serpent? God gave man the freedom to choose. When God confronted him, Adam blamed Eve and Eve blamed the devil and neither accepted the responsibility for disobeying God. Not much has changed. We blame friends, parents, home, environment, circumstances—anyone but ourselves.

It's a hard lesson but children must be taught to accept responsibility for their actions rather than blame others. They have to understand that if they commit wrong acts they will suffer the consequences. When they don't accept blame, their destructive behavior can go unchecked and things can go from bad to worse. If you allow kids to place blame, you're stetting in motion a vicious circle of behavior.

People who blame are basically insecure, have low self-esteem and do not really like themselves. This may be the result when children have been excessively criticized and resort to blaming as a means of defending themselves. It is very important that parents avoid disciplining their children in front of others whenever possible. Little good and much harm come from embarrassing, humiliating and stripping children of their dignity. "Fathers [and mothers] do not provoke your children, lest they become discouraged."

It is very easy to fall into the trap of making excuses to rationalize behavior. Resist the temptation to blame and thereby set a good example for your children. Teach them to accept responsibility for their actions and not resort to making excuses and blaming others. It's a grave injustice to overlook irresponsible behavior in children and bail them out rather than letting them face the consequences of their actions.

Blessings

Theologian Herbert W. Armstrong has made the following proclamation: "Can you realize that every unhappiness, every evil that has come to humanity has been the result of transgressing God's law."

"If no one every had any other god before the true God; if all children were reared to honor, respect and obey their parents, and all parents reared their children in God's ways; if no one ever allowed the spirit of murder to enter his heart, if there were no wars, no killing of humans by humans; if all marriages were kept happy and there were no transgressions of chastity before or after marriage; if all had so much concern for the good and welfare of others that no one would steal—and we could throw away all locks, keys and safes; if everyone told the truth—everyone's word were good—everyone were honest; if no one ever coveted what was not rightfully his, but had so much outgoing concern for the welfare of others that he really believed it is more blessed to *give* than to receive—what a happy world we would have!

"In such a world, with all loving and worshiping God with all their minds, hearts and strength—with all having concern for the welfare of all others equal to concern for self—there would be no divorce—no broken homes or families, no juvenile delinquency, no crime, no jails or prisons, no police except for peaceful direction and supervision as a public service for all, no wars, no military establishments.

"But, further, God has set in motion physical laws that operate in our bodies and minds, as well as the spiritual law. There would be no sickness, ill health, pain or suffering. There would be, on the contrary, vigorous, vibrant good health, filled with dynamic interest in life, enthusiastic interest in constructive activities bringing happiness and joy. There would be cleanliness, vigorous activity, real progress, no slums, no degenerate backward races or areas of earth."

Blessing for Obedience: "If you fully obey the Lord your God and carefully follow all His commands I give you today, the Lord your God will set you high above all the nations on earth." Deuteronomy 28: 1-2.

"Now picture the changed conditions! Look now at the solved problems! See, now, a glimpse into a world of no illiteracy, no poverty, no famine and starvation, into a world where crime decreases rapidly, people learn honesty, chastity, human kindness and happiness—a world of peace, prosperity, abundant well-being."

Busy People

Satan called a worldwide convention. In his opening address to his evil angels, he said, "We can't keep the Christians from going to church. We can't keep them from reading their Bibles and knowing the truth. We can't even keep them from forming an intimate, abiding relationship experience in Christ. If they gain that connection with Jesus, our power over them is broken.

"So let them go to their churches, let them have their conservative lifestyles, but steal their time, so they can't gain that relationship with Jesus Christ. This is what I want you to do, angels. Distract them from gaining hold of their Savior and maintaining that vital connection throughout their day!"

"How shall we do this?" shouted his angels. "Keep them busy in the non-essentials of life and invent innumerable schemes to occupy their minds," he answered. "Tempt them to spend, spend, spend and borrow, borrow, borrow. Persuade the wives to go to work for long hours and the husbands to work six to seven days a week, ten to twelve hours a day, so they can afford their empty lifestyles. Keep them from spending time with their children. As their family fragments, soon their home will offer no escape from the pressures of work!

"Over-stimulate their minds so that they cannot hear that still, small voice. Entice them to play the radio or cassette player whenever they drive and to keep the TV, VCR, CDs and their PCs going constantly in their homes. And see to it that every store and restaurant in the world plays non-biblical music constantly. This will jam their minds and break that union with Christ.

"Fill the coffee table with magazines and newspapers. Pound their minds with the news 24 hours a day. Invade their driving moments with billboards. Flood their mailboxes with junk mail, mail-order catalogues, sweepstakes, services and false hopes. Keep skinny, beautiful models on the magazines so the husbands will believe that external beauty is what's important, and they'll become dissatisfied with their wives. Ha! That will fragment those families quickly!

"Even in their recreation, let them be excessive. Have them return from their recreation exhausted, disquieted and unprepared for the coming week. Don't let them go out in nature to reflect on God's wonders. Send them to amusement parks, sporting events, concerts and movies instead. Keep them busy, busy, busy! And when they meet for spiritual fellowship, involve them in gossip and small talk so that they leave with troubled consciences and unsettled emotion.

"Go ahead, let them be involved in soul-winning. But crowd their lives with so many good causes they have no time to seek power from Christ. Soon they will be working in their own strength, sacrificing their health and family for the good of the cause. It will work! It will work!"

It was a quiet convention. And the evil angels went eagerly to their assignments causing Christians everywhere to get busy, busy, busy and to rush here and there.

I guess the question is, "Has the Devil been successful at his scheme?" You be the judge!

B—Being
U—Under
S—Satan's
Y—Yoke

Are you **BUSY**?

—Author Unknown

Character

Character consists of a combination of emotional, intellectual and ethical traits that distinguishes one person (or group) from another. A person with good character is accountable, caring, fair, honest, kind, loving, sincere, trustworthy and more. If practicing these principles produces positive results (and they do), then the consequences of doing the opposite most surely will generate negative results.

Character is much easier to define than live out. At the risk of oversimplifying, building good character is simply a matter of teaching and practicing right from wrong, and it doesn't happen over a short period of time. Nothing we could think, say or do comes even close to being as important as good character, and there is a devastating price to pay for underdeveloped character.

So, when does character count? Character counts in the home. Character development is the primary responsibility of parents. If good character traits are not instilled in children early, often they are not learned at all. Here is where seeds of personal conduct and acceptable behavior are planted. Be responsible! Tell the truth! Respect your elders! Mind your manners! Treat others the way you want to be treated! And so on. Too often, parents place more emphasis on what children achieve rather than how they learn and interact with others. Good character development will not be quick and easy. It requires that children be closely supervised until maturity.

Character counts in school. Parents can no longer rely on the school system to teach good character as it once did. Character development is no longer top priority. The culture has replaced it with its own version. Much behavior once considered inappropriate is now acceptable. Situation ethics now dominate and dictate what is considered proper behavior. Many absolute standards have become obsolete — a thing of the past. Adults and children alike need to take advantage of every opportunity to determine the differences between right and wrong and expect to pay the price when they deviate from these principles.

Character counts in the workplace. As valuable as knowledge of the job and training are, character is even more important. For example, traits that employers look for in their employees are honesty, dependability, reliability, punctuality, and the ability to get along with other employees by treating them the same way they want to be treated. Proper conduct does matter because it is the number one reason employees are not promoted or are fired.

Character counts in leadership. Look at the present generation and you see the character of our future leaders. Our national character is an accumulation of the principles and virtues practiced in our personal lives, homes, schools, workplaces, neighborhoods and positions of leadership, including the President of the United States. Leaders at all levels of society must set the example and serve as role models for future leaders. The character displayed by each citizen contributes to our national character for better or worse.

Character building is a continuous process. It is important to know that even small character flaws left unchecked can have seriously negative consequences. Good character traits must be an active force in the lives of everyone. When this is not the case, someone will get hurt. Every person alive is affected by the actions of others at some time, in some way, in some place.

An upright character is of greatest worth. It cannot be bought. The formation of a noble character is the work of a lifetime and can only be the result of diligent and persevering effort. Good character is what we look for in others and it is what others look for in us. So, when does character count? Character always counts!

Children and School

By the time children are old enough to start school, they have come a long way and learned a great deal. They have done much of it on their own with parents as their teachers. Parents need to teach their children right from wrong and instill character traits, such as honesty, fairness, respect, honor, loyalty, kindness, dependability and manners.

Good students come to school ready to learn. Specifically, what does that mean? Good students do what's important:

- pay attention, listen and concentrate
- follow classroom rules
- raise their hand before speaking
- participate and ask questions

Parents need to remind their children why school is important. They are there to learn to speak correctly, read, write, learn math, communicate, understand and be understood. Good students have specific goals, such as experiencing success, learning to be independent, and becoming law-abiding adults.

Few parents realize how much their children have learned by age six. They have become gender-conscious. They have acquired almost two-thirds of their height. They will be one-third of the way toward being practically on their own. Some child experts say that by age six, children will have learned over half of their life-guiding principles for living, especially behavior-wise. Most of the seeds that influence behavior will have been planted. The kind of fruit they will bear, during the remaining school years and the rest of their lives, will result from these seeds.

Although many parents tend to blame the schools when their children don't do well, in reality, the schools are simply a reflection of the homes from which students come. They must accept the fact that it is they, and not the school, who are ultimately responsible for how their children turn out. They are the most important teachers their children will ever have. It is their example and caring that will be the major influence on the attitude, accomplishments and behavior of their children.

Parents must realize that children differ in their abilities and this will be reflected in their performance at different age levels. That is why it is so important for parents to get to know them individually. Children tend to do their best even though at times it might not appear that way. Parents should avoid comparing their children with other children, especially brothers and sisters. It is best when children compete against themselves. By doing this they can see their progress and find satisfaction in it. Children need to experience success or else they will give up and stop trying.

One of the areas that parents and educators need to examine more closely is the age at which children are permitted to start school. Attendance laws vary from state to state. Most school districts allow children to enroll as late as September closest to their sixth birthday (fifth for kindergarten). The assumption is that when children's birthdays fall in this range, they are all ready to start school physically, mentally and socially. Nothing could be further from reality.

Even children born on the same day differ. Children don't walk, talk, toilet train, or have the same interests at the same time. Therefore, it is unlikely that they would all be ready to do all that would be expected of them in school.

There are many possible reasons performance varies among children. Differences are a major factor: age, intelligence, background, abilities, proper discipline, right attitude, and degree of maturity, especially the differences between girls, who tend to mature earlier, and boys, to mention a few.

When all these factors are taken into consideration—children who are younger because of birth date; children who differ in mental development; and the maturity differences between girls and boys—we are talking about a possible three-year age difference in the same classroom. Add to that the fact that they could be sitting next to each other.

Allowing children to start school before they are ready often leads to a continuous struggle of playing "catch up." In many instances it may mean the difference between liking or hating school. In my experience as a teacher and guidance counselor for thirty-three years, I found that three out of four younger boys and one out of four younger girls encountered serious difficulties at school. The younger boys and girls who do succeed are usually above average in intelligence and come from above average home environments. Even in these cases, one can't help wondering whether they would have done even better with students their own age.

Age is not a perfect method to determine when children should start school; however, it is unlikely to change in the near future. My recommendation is that children who turn six in June or later of that year (five for kindergarten) would be wise to wait until the following September to enroll. This means that all first-graders will then turn seven (six for kindergarten) by the end of the school year. Whereas now, the June, July, August and September birthdays (one-third of first-graders and one-third of kindergarteners) respectively are still six and five by the end of the school year. It is to the student's advantage to be one of the older rather than younger members of the class, especially boys.

There are other long-term consequences and considerations. Many children younger than their classmates tend to struggle in school and end up with a poor self-image. If immaturity is the problem, the gap will widen more each year and achievement will continue to drop off. When children can't or don't keep up, they often will be teased about it. Poor school performance becomes a constant source of bickering and frustration at home and in school. Grade levels dictate expectations forcing students into social situations before they are really ready: sports, dances, proms, dating, etc. When younger students go out for sports, they have to compete against older classmates. Younger students may be at a disadvantage when taking college entrance and scholarship tests and managing on their own away from home. Later is better!

Consequences

Consequences are the results of actions taken by people based on their definition of right and wrong. The differences are beyond one's imagination. On the one hand are those who say, "Treat me the way I want to be treated." On the other hand are those who say, "Treat me the way you want to be treated." Everyone else falls somewhere between these two extremes. Who's right? Who's wrong?

Although many people disagree with the numerous aspects of what's right and what's wrong, they do agree that society could not survive without laws that define some form of right from wrong behavior. Obviously, this is why laws that conform to accepted standards of right and wrong and have endured the test of time have been established and put in place.

History records that when people keep the established moral and civil laws, the consequences are positive. When people fail to keep these established laws, the consequences are negative. Each person is held responsible for deciding which road to take and what choices to make. The consequences will certainly be there. Those choosing to break the law will be found guilty and suffer the negative consequences. Those choosing to obey the law will be found innocent and experience the positive consequences.

Negative behavior produces negative consequences. Positive behavior produces positive consequences. We reap what we sow. It can't be any other way! The time span between the actions and the consequences will often vary. In fact, it's possible that they may not become known in one's lifetime. But, one thing is certain: someone, some time, somewhere will inherit the consequences.

To what degree people abide by civil and moral laws will determine whether the consequences of their actions will be positive or negative. The following character traits are just a sampling of the hundreds of moral principles and guidelines by which people live: abusive, anxious, envious, generous, grateful, greedy, honest, kind, loving, patient, promiscuous, successful. Readers are encouraged to analyze and determine what effects they might have in their lives and then apply these insights to the many other facets of their lives. What determines which road you travel on your journey of life? What is your moral compass?

Everyone subscribes to some kind of guiding force or god to determine what's right or wrong for them: atheism, fame, humanism, money, popularity, power, secularism, success, witchcraft, to name a few. What one chooses to value most becomes his or her god.

Just as following natural laws, such as gravity, protects us from physical harm, obeying civil and moral laws shields us from much of life's needless suffering. This makes it more possible for us to live more meaningful, constructive and productive lives.

The guiding light for this essay is the Bible, particularly the Ten Commandments. Martin Luther (1483-1546) said, "Every thought, word, and deed contrary to God's Law is sin; all evil in the world is the consequence of man's sinning."

1. You shall have no other gods before me.

2. You shall not make for yourself an idol.

3. You shall not take the name of the Lord your God in vain.

4. Remember the Sabbath day by keeping it holy.

5. Honor your father and your mother.

6. You shall not murder.

7. You shall not commit adultery.

8. You shall not steal.

9. You shall not give false testimony against your neighbor.

10. You shall not covet.

When asked which commandment is greatest, Jesus said, "You shall love the Lord your God with all your heart, and with all your soul, and with all your mind." This is the greatest and first commandment. And a second is like it: "You shall love your neighbor [any person with whom one comes in contact] as yourself." The key word in living is LOVE.

Contentment

Contentment is the state of being satisfied with the present situation. It's not necessarily wealth, material possessions or positive circumstances, although they can contribute to it. The world is filled with disappointed people longing for contentment, but "things" don't guarantee it. How do we know? Because millions of people have all these things and are not content; and there are many who possess much less and are.

Our pursuit of contentment is the driving force in almost all that we do. There is no limit to the sacrifices we make and the pain we endure to gain it. Contentment is a real mystery. You can't see it or touch it and no one has really defined it. But, those who possess it, treasure it and those who don't often spend the greater part of their lives searching for it.

How do we acquire contentment? Before elaborating on this question, I want to comment on the difference between contentment and happiness. Happiness results from a particular event or occurrence and is usually short-lived at best. On the other hand, contentment may or may not include happy moments and/or circumstances but not rely on them for contentment.

Contentment is realized and experienced best when we apply Godly principles to our expectations, desires and wishes. Only then will we feel truly satisfied with our possessions, status and circumstances. Contentment reflects satisfaction with what we have and what we are at this point in our lives regardless of what our future hopes may be. "Be content with such things as you have." The world is filled with disappointed people seeking contentment from worldly, material possessions. Contentment is rooted in what people are and not in what they have.

25

Another key to the contented life is to look upward and not inward. The apostle Paul is a good example of such an approach to living. He chose to live his life in accordance with God's will. In spite of his many trials, he managed to live the contented life as noted in the following passage: "For I have learned in whatever state I am, to be content: I know how to be abased and I know how to abound. Everywhere and in all things I have learned both to be full and to be hungry, both to abound and to suffer need. I can do all things through Christ who strengthens me."

When people understand the value of God's love, they will then discover His peace and joy, no matter what the circumstances that surround them. If living each minute, hour and day is devoted to the following biblical principles, then each day will be one of contentment. As challenging as this may seem, it is very comforting to know that "with God all things are possible."

Contentment is a state of mind that depends almost entirely on the individual. We often depend on others and/or circumstances for our contentment, but this is seldom the way it is. Each person is responsible and accountable for his or her degree of contentment or discontentment. It's a matter of attitude. The truly contented person is one who can be as enthusiastic about the things one is required to do as well as the things one wants to do.

In the words of Billy Graham, "The happiness for which our souls ache is one undisturbed by success or failure, one which will root deeply inside us and give inward relaxation, peace, and contentment, no matter what the surface problems may be." Contentment is a wonderful thing. It is one of the most precious gifts that we can give to ourselves as well as to wish for others.

Contrasting Values

- All virtue is loving right, all sin is loving wrong.

- A man is rich according to what he is, not according to what he has.

- A man who both spends and saves money is the happiest man, because he has both enjoyments.

- An attitude of gratitude focuses on the positive rather than the negative.

- A person of words and not deeds is like a garden full of weeds.

- A pessimist sees the difficulty in every opportunity; an optimist sees the opportunity in every difficulty.

- As a rule, none of us can see ourselves as others see us, and others cannot see us as we see ourselves.

- Darkness cannot drive out darkness; only light can do that.

- Dodge responsibilities, and get hit by consequences.

- Does your employer consider you profit or overhead?

- Do not conform any longer to the pattern of this world, but be transformed to the renewing of your mind.

- Either the Bible will keep you away from sin, or sin will keep you away from the Bible.

- Everyone loves himself most, but wants others to love him more than they love themselves.

- For most people trying to find the road to success, breaking the rules is a shortcut to failure.

- He is a wise man who does not grieve for the things, which he has not, but rejoices for those which he has.

- If you aren't sure something is right, ask yourself what most people would do, then do the opposite.

- It is better to fail in a cause that will ultimately succeed than to succeed in a cause that will ultimately fail.

- Learning from the past has taken a backseat to learning from the present.

- Many believe that there are no absolutes because everything is relative.

- Many people are indifferent to right or wrong because of value relativism.

- No man was ever honored for what he received. Honor has been the reward for what he gave.

- Remember change and change for the better are two different things. Stand for something or you'll fall for anything.

- The gap between liberals and conservatives has become so wide that neither can be trusted.

- The louder parents talk to their children, the less that they listen. The opposite tends to be true as well.

- Things turn our best for the people who make the best of the way things turn out.

- There's my truth, your truth, and the truth.

- Two people can look at the same thing and see it differently.

- We can control only one thing in our lives, and that's our attitude.

- We reap what we sow: it's so obvious that people don't believe it.

- You can give without loving, but you can't love without giving.
- You can't unscramble an egg, but you can make an omlette.

Culture Changes

Culture consists of certain characteristics that an individual or a group of people have in common. This then evolves into a way of life that becomes known as society or civilization. There is much concern today by many people of just how far our society has drifted from the principles that founded and guided our nation for 234 years.

Over a period of time a culture might remain the same, improve or decline. Some of those changes could impact our society in a negative way; they include personal appearance, behavior, family, non-parental influence, school and sexuality.

> **Personal Appearance:** conformity, earring place-ment, indiscreet dress, makeup, dyed hair, tattoos.

> **Behavior:** drug and alcohol abuse, immediate grati-fication, situational ethics, susceptibility to fads, van-dalism, vulgar talk.

> **Family:** less church attendance, disobedience, divorce, fatherlessness/single motherhood, lack of manners, obesity.

> **Non-parental Influence:** Internet, peer pressure, sexting, smart phones, television, video games.

> **School:** absentees, dropouts, lack of after-school supervision, low test scores, no moral instruction, school violence.

> **Sexuality:** homosexuality, pornography, promiscuous sex, same sex marriage, sexually transmitted diseases, unwanted pregnancy.

Each category above could generate a discussion in itself. Family, for example, is the very foundation upon which society rests. It is the first and often the only place where children are nurtured, loved and accepted for what they are, in an environment where they can learn principles and values that will help equip them for adulthood. Children can sense when family comes first and this realization will bring out the best in them. They thrive when parents exercise strong leadership; this tells them they are loved and thereby more receptive to instruction and guidance. Children especially should be taught to think twice before following the crowd. A passage from the Book of Matthew, 7:13-14, says, "Wide is the gate and broad is the road that leads to destruction, and many enter through it. But small is the gate and narrow the road that leads to life, and only a few find it."

In our culture, we often discover too late that what we thought was right turns out to be wrong and what we thought was wrong turns out to be right. The test for a right decision is: Did it adhere to biblical truth? Though a particular choice may seem right at the time, if biblical standards are ignored, eventually the foolishness of that choice will become evident with negative consequences sure to follow.

It also should be noted that history is filled with great civilizations that have come and gone, all experiencing moral decay from within. Historian Edward Gibbon (1737-94) listed five major causes for the decline and fall of the Roman Empire:

1. The rapid increase of divorce: the undermining of the dignity and sanctity of the home, which is the basis of human society.

2. Increasingly higher taxes and the spending of public money for free bread and circuses for the populace.

3. The mad craze for pleasure: sports becoming every year more exciting and more brutal.

4. The building of gigantic armaments when the real enemy was within, the decadence of the people.

5. The decay of religion: faith fading into mere form, losing touch with life and becoming less important to guide the people.

History does not document one civilization that survived without a dominating number of morally strong families. How would you rate the moral state of America today? Has our culture changed for the better—or the worse?

Death: Heaven or Hell?

Death is the most certain thing in life and often prepared for the least. The soul is that part of one's being that is thought of as who we really are. It continues after physical death and leaves the body intact to eternal life in Heaven [paradise] or Hell [torment]. God makes this judgment based on the only thing that accompanies us—our character—not on the inventory that we leave behind.

"There shall be a resurrection of the dead, both of the just and unjust." This is biblical truth. One may choose not to believe it but that doesn't make it any less true.

What happens to people after they die? Everyone must answer this question for himself or herself and their children when they ask. The Bible answer is clear beyond doubt. Believers: those who believe and trust in Jesus as their Lord and Savior will spend eternity with Him in Heaven. Nonbelievers: those who choose a different path will spend eternity separated from Him in Hell. It is one or the other. People are free to believe or not believe and live and die with the consequences of that choice. I agree with those who think a measure of Heaven and Hell is experienced while we are still living on this earth.

On what basis do people make the greatest decision they will ever make? The Bible teaches that there are two kinds of birth: physical birth, which we have nothing to do with, and spiritual birth, which we have everything to do with. "Unless one is born again [the second birth] he [she] cannot experience the Kingdom of God. That which is born of the flesh is flesh, and that which is born of the Spirit is spirit." The flesh dies but the spirit lives in eternity.

The second birth is not something that we inherit from our parents. It's a choice and decision that each person must make for himself or herself when they feel called to do so. The rebirth experience is a gradual unfolding process that continues throughout life, much like babies mature into adulthood. Then God opens their eyes to a different lifestyle with new meaning and purpose. Their way of living will develop in the direction that their spiritual birth leads them. They will become more God-centered and less self-centered, learning to do more in what is right in God's sight.

Salvation is our greatest need. Why? Because we are all born with a sinful nature and because of this we are hostile and antagonistic toward God. We want to do it our way instead of God's way. The end result is sin. Sin is the act of disobeying God's laws, intentionally or unintentionally. It's worth noting that often we are not punished for our sins, but rather because of their consequences.

So, what's the solution? To the believer, God's word in the Book of Romans equips us with a simple, clear and foolproof plan: **Admit you are a sinner.** "For all have sinned and come short of the glory of God." 3:23; **Believe that Jesus Christ died for your sins.** "But God demonstrates His love toward us, in that, while we were yet sinners, Christ died for us." 5:8; **Commit your life to Jesus.** "For whosoever shall call upon the name of the Lord shall be saved." 10:13.

According to the Bible, those who decide to reject Jesus as Savior are destined to spend eternity in Hell; however, those who decide to accept Jesus as Savior are destined to spend eternity in Heaven. It's your/our call.

Denominationalism

Denominations are religious groups that have much in common and assemble for worship. They may refer to themselves as an assembly, congregation, or by a specified church name, such as those noted below, none of which appear in the Bible.

The National Council of Church's report (based on a 2009 survey) on church membership lists the following organizations as the top ten biggest religious denominations in the USA:

1. The Catholic Church: 68.5 million
2. Southern Baptist Convention: 16.1 million
3. The United Methodist Church: 7.8 million
4. The Church of Jesus Christ of Latter-day Saints: 6 million
5. The Church of God in Christ: 5.5 million
6. National Baptist Convention, USA: 5 million
7. Evangelical Lutheran Church in America: 4.5 million
8. National Baptist Convention of America: 3.5 million
9. Assemblies of God: 2.9 million
10. Presbyterian Church (USA): 2.7 million

The Cleveland phone book lists over 100 denominations and 200 independent churches.

Today in America seventy-five percent of adults identify themselves as Christian. In comparison, the next largest religions in America are Islam and Judaism. Combined they represent only one to two percent of the USA population. However, there are more than 1,500 different Christian faith groups in America. (Which one is right?)

Christianity is ranked as the largest religion in the world today with approximately 2 billion adherents. Thirty-three percent of the world's population is considered to be Christian, and there are approximately 38,000 Christian denominations. This statistic takes into consideration cultural distinctions of denominations in different countries. The Roman Catholic Church is the largest Christian group today with more than a billion followers constituting about half of the world's Christian population. (Reference: World Christian Encyclopedia)

Denominations differ on a variety of issues, including Biblical interpretation, customs and traditions; social issues of birth control, abortion and homosexuality; clergy; heaven, hell and purgatory; sacraments (baptism, communion, etc.); saints, sinners and salvation (faith alone or good works, spiritual second birth); tithing (gross, net); and when and how to worship.

In the last 2,000 years America has gone from one Christian denomination (The Church of God, the only church name recorded in the Bible) to more than 1,500 different denominations and cults. Could the following be some negative consequences from this evolution: a decrease in church attendance (about one in three attend church services); over half of all marriages end in divorce; half of all babies are born out of wedlock; a weakening of the family; a decline in moral values? One could conclude that denominations with closer attention to Biblical principles would be a major step in the right direction.

No church is perfect because all of its members (no matter the hierarchy) are imperfect due to man's sinful nature. All violate God's laws to one degree or another. It's time for members of all denominations to focus on what they have in common rather than on their differences and learn from one another. The closer an individual, group or church parallels the Bible, the better equipped they will be to distinguish right from wrong. Mark Twain, who didn't consider himself religious, said, "Some people claim they are troubled by parts of the Bible which they cannot understand. What troubles me is that part of the Bible which I understand only too well."

Jesus summarized the total Bible message very simply: "Love the Lord your God with all your *heart* and with all your *soul* and with all your *mind*. This is the first and greatest commandment. And the second is like it. Love your neighbor as yourself." Matthew 22:37-39. Let's try to keep it simple and find common ground.

Desiderata

Go placidly amid the noise and the haste, and remember what peace there may be in silence.

As far as possible, without surrender, be on good terms with all persons. Speak your truth quietly and clearly; and listen to others, even to the dull and the ignorant; they too have their story.

Avoid loud and aggressive persons; they are vexatious to the spirit.

If you compare yourself with others, you may become vain or bitter, for always there will be greater and lesser persons than yourself.

Enjoy your achievements as well as your plans. Keep interested in your own career, however humble; it is a real possession in the changing fortunes of time.

Exercise caution in your business affairs, for the world is full of trickery. But let this not blind you to what virtue there is; many persons strive for high ideals, and everywhere life is full of heroism.

Be yourself. Especially do not feign affection. Neither be cynical about love, for in the face of all aridity and disenchantment, it is as perennial as the grass.

Take kindly the counsel of the years, gracefully surrendering the things of youth. Nurture strength of spirit to shield you in sudden misfortune. But do not distress yourself with dark imaginings. Many fears are born of fatigue and loneliness.

Beyond a wholesome discipline, be gentle with yourself. You are a child of the universe no less than the trees and the stars; you have a right to be here.

And whether or not it is clear to you, no doubt the universe is unfolding as it should. Therefore be at peace with God, whatever you conceive Him to be; and whatever your labors and aspirations, in the noisy confusion of life, keep peace in your soul.

With all its sham, drudgery, and broken dreams, it is still a beautiful world. Be cheerful. Strive to be happy.

—Max Ehrmann

Diligence

Faith is the root of the Christian way of life. It requires nourishment, and one of the main nutrients to nourish faith is diligence. In fact, it demands it! Diligence means to proceed in one's undertaking in a careful, steady, persistent and understanding way. In the words of writer Henry M. Morris, Ph.D., each person is commanded to "Be diligent in diligence!"

On what are we to focus our diligence? Seven guiding principles that will help produce a well-rounded, fruitful Christian life are recorded in the Bible in Second Peter, Chapter One. They are designed to nurture our faith in God's word and include the following:

Virtue (goodness, justice, moral excellence);

Knowledge (comprehension, Scripture, understanding);

Temperance (abstinence, moderation, perseverance);

Patience (calmness, endurance, steadfastness);

Godliness (devotion, holiness, reverence);

Brotherly Kindness (friendship, mercy, tolerance);

Charity (affection, Christian love, forgiveness).

The above listing, as important as it is, is far from exhaustive; also, it goes without saying that to what degree people practice these principles will vary from person to person in accordance with his or her age, maturity level and giftedness. Fortunately, salvation becomes a reality by belief and faith in Christ as our personal Savior by grace, not our works.

By way of illustration and encouragement, visualize yourself as a newborn baby, and how, with loving care, proper support and steadfast patience, adulthood becomes a reality. This same scenario is just as applicable to the Christian way of life.

Practicing the above principles to the best of one's ability should influence an individual's attitudes, actions and relationships in a positive direction. The Bible encourages us to "Love one another deeply, because love covers a multitude of sins."

Discover the Bible

The Bible is a library of sacred writings that reveals GOD'S WORD dating back thousands of years before Christ. It was written over a 1,500-year period by 40 authors in three different languages on three continents, in ten countries, in 1,551 places, depicting 2,930 characters, and without any contradictions.

The Bible contains 66 books divided into two parts: the Old Testament with 39 books (about 593,000 words) beginning with creation and continuing with the history and prophecies of the Nation of Israel. The New Testament with 27 books (about 180,000 words) focuses on the birth, life, death, and resurrection of Jesus and the work of his disciples during the first century AD.

A proper understanding of the Scriptures requires the study of the complete book. This will reveal its overall theme: God's claim to rule mankind and to make known His loving purpose to everyone.

The Bible is more than a historical document to be preserved. Its language is plain, direct, and meaningful. It touches on geography, history, science, philosophy, ethics—in fact, every area of human thought including marriage, family, and friends. Although God's prophets and followers of Jesus wrote the actual words, God directed their thoughts, making it His infallible and authoritative WORD. The Bible covers it all.

"All Scripture is God-breathed (God's active involvement) and is useful for teaching, rebuking, correcting, and training in righteousness, so that the man of God may be thoroughly equipped for every good work." 2 Timothy 3:16.

The Bible's record of fulfilled prophecy is perfect. Here are just a few examples:

- Fall of Babylon...Isaiah 47:1

- Birth of Christ in Bethlehem…Micah 5:2
- Rise and Fall of Greece…Daniel 8:1
- Born of a Virgin…Isaiah 7:14
- Out of Egypt I Called my Son…Hosea 11:1
- Sold for 30 Pieces of Silver…Zechariah 11:12

  Fulfilled prophecy and all the recorded miracles serve as conclusive evidence that the Bible is divine in nature and not something humans invented.

  The Bible is unquestionably the most important book in history. Two thousand years have passed since its last recorded words. Unlike other books, it has never dwindled into oblivion. Here's what some have said about it:

- "A man's word is a little sound that flies into the air and soon vanishes; but the word of God endures everlastingly." Martin Luther, 1483-1546.

- "Unless God's word illumines the way, the whole life of men is wrapped in darkness and mist, so that they cannot but miserably stray." —John Calvin, 1509-1564.

- "It is impossible to rightly govern the world without God and the Bible." —George Washington, 1732-1799.

- "Nobody ever outgrows the Scripture; the Book widens and deepens with our years." —Charles Spurgeon, 1858-1892.

- "A thorough knowledge of the Bible is worth more than a college education." —Theodore Roosevelt, 1858-1905.

Even though the Bible remains the most controversial book ever written, it continues to be a living source of instruction. It spells out right from wrong. It clearly reveals the consequences when people obey or disobey it.

God's word is for all people because it speaks to the human condition. Bible surveys indicate that more than 90% of all Americans own at least one Bible, but fewer than half actually read it; and even fewer allow it to affect their daily living.

The Bible is in a class of its own. Year after year, more copies than any other book are printed, circulated, and translated into over 2,000 languages. It speaks to the small child, yet challenges the greatest intellects. The New Testament records the events and sayings of Jesus and the work of his Apostles. He is by far the most significant and influential person in the Bible and the world. Jesus has positively impacted every aspect of human life.

"He was born in an obscure village. He worked in a carpenter shop until he was thirty. He then became an itinerant preacher. He never held an office. He never had a family or owned a house. He didn't go to college. He had no credentials but himself. He was only thirty-three when the pubic turned against him. His friends ran away. He was turned over to his enemies and went through the mockery of a trial. He was nailed to a cross between two thieves. While he was dying, his executioners gambled for his clothing, the only property he had on earth. He was laid in a borrowed grave.

"Two thousand centuries have come and gone, and today he is the central figure of the human race. All the armies that ever marched, and all the navies that ever sailed, all the parliaments that ever sat, and all the kings that ever reigned, have not affected the lives of man on this earth as much as that ONE SOLITARY LIFE." —Anonymous

"For God so loved the world that He gave His only Son, that whoever believes in Him should not perish but have eternal life." —John: 3:16

God loves sinners but hates sin. Jesus invites all to repent of their sins and accept His death on the cross as the ultimate sacrifice to rescue people from their sins—something they cannot do for themselves.

Those who believe and trust Jesus as Lord and Savior will inherit eternal life in heaven (present with God). Those who do not, will inherit eternal life in Hell (absent from God). It is one or the other. The Bible teaches that salvation is achieved solely by God's grace and not our own merit, although good works tend to follow.

In summary, the Bible contains the following:

- The mind of God, the state of man, the way of salvation, the doom of sinners, and the happiness of believers.

- Its doctrines are holy, its precepts are binding, its histories are true, and its decisions are immutable.

- Read it to be wise, believe it to be safe, and practice it to be holy.

- It contains light to direct you, food to support you, and comfort to cheer you. It is the traveler's map, the pilgrim's staff, the pilot's compass, the soldier's sword, and the Christian's charter.

- Here Paradise is restored, Heaven opened, and the gates of Hell disclosed. Christ is its grand subject, our good its design, and the glory of God its end.

- It should fill the memory, rule the heart and guide the feet. Read it slowly, frequently, prayerfully.

- It is a mine of wealth, a paradise of glory, and a river of pleasure. It is given to you in life, will be opened at the judgment, and be remembered forever.

- It involves the highest responsibility, will reward the greatest labor, and condemn all who trifle with its sacred contents.

For those not familiar with the Bible, the Gospel of John is a good place to start. It has 29 pages and 21 chapters that average 42 verses. Use the New International Version (NIV) translation. Other books to explore include James, Ruth, Acts, Philippians and Luke.

Education

There is much concern today about the negative trends in education in America: decline in educational standards, drop in standardized achievement test scores, severe discipline problems, unexcused tardiness and absences, vandalism, theft, cheating, lying, drug abuses and promiscuity, to mention a few.

In a November 2010 speech, Secretary of Education Arne Duncan reported that "one-quarter of U. S. high school students drop out or fail to graduate on time. Almost one million students leave our schools for the streets each year."

About this same time a group of top retired generals and admirals released the following information: "Seventy-five percent of young Americans, between the ages of 17 to 24, are unable to enlist in the military today because they have failed to graduate from high school, have a criminal record, or are physically unfit. America's youth are now tied for ninth in the world in college attainment."

Duncan has initiated several reforms to achieve the highest educational standards. His biggest push is to raise the status of the teaching profession. Why?

Tony Wagner, the Harvard-based education expert and author of *The Global Achievement Gap*, explains it this way. "There are three basic skills that students need if they want to thrive in a knowledge economy: the ability to do critical thinking and problem-solving, the ability to communicate effectively, and the ability to collaborate."

Two of the countries that lead in these skills are Finland and Denmark. They insist that their teachers come from the top one-third of their college graduating class. As Wagner put it, "They took teaching from an assembly-line job to a knowledge-worker's job. They have invested massively in how they recruit, train and support teachers, to attract and retain the best."

I certainly agree that the recruitment of teachers needs to be upgraded. After devoting thirty-three years to the educational system of America as a teacher and counselor, I'm of the opinion that one-fourth of the teachers do an excellent job, one-half do an adequate job, and one-fourth do a poor job.

Thomas L. Friedman, columnist for *The New York Times,* in an article titled "Teaching for America" is in total agreement with Duncan and Wagner and adds: "All good ideas, but if we want better teachers, we also need better parents—parents who turn off the TV and video games, make sure homework is completed, encourage reading and elevate learning as the most important life skill. The more we demand from teachers, the more we have to demand from students and parents. That's the contract for America that will truly ensure our national security."

I would add another skill to those of Duncan, Wagner and Friedman: moral principles that spell out right and wrong behavior. Ethics is the process by which these determinations are made; for the Godly, the process is always God-centered rather than self-centered where anything goes.

Children need moral standards to make the right behavioral choices. Godly principles provide and equip them with those standards. Parents who rear their children by God's laws can rest assured that they will serve them throughout their lives.

God holds parents responsible for teaching their children right and wrong. Teaching moral principles is an ongoing process, and that is why it's so important for parents to be with their children as much as possible, especially during the formative years.

In children's eyes, their parents are God. So, before parents can teach their children about the God they want them to follow, they must make sure that they are representing Him accurately in their own lives. Chances are children are going to worship the God of their parents, whoever or whatever it is.

Expectations

What do you expect of your children? Think long and hard so that you don't put undue pressure on them. Unrealistic expectations can be a source of much irritation and disappointment for both parents and children. The wider the gap between what parents think and the actual facts, the greater the unhappiness. When children get the message that nothing they do is quite good enough, they soon view themselves as failures and conduct themselves accordingly.

It is important that parents have reasonable, realistic and fair expectations for their children. When they do not, children live in fear of the consequences of disappointing their parents. This ought not be. When children cannot please their parents, they often resort to making excuses in order to survive. Making excuses in one area may carry over to other areas and be adopted as a way of coping in the family.

It becomes easier and easier to make excuses rather than try to meet even the attainable expectations. This teaches children to be dishonest. If they cannot be honest with their parents and themselves, they surely will not be honest with others. Children who become good at making excuses seldom become good at anything else. Basically, children really do want to please their parents.

When parental expectations are self-directed rather than God-directed, disappointment, frustration and unhappiness are sure to follow for both parents and children. "In all your ways acknowledge Him, and He shall direct your paths." God has provided His complete infallible Word as a guide for parenting. God is to parents what parents are to children. Once they know what God expects of them, their expectations for their children will be appropriate. And what God expects of them is to make the best use of their talents. It

49

is cruel to expect behavior from children they are incapable of giving. There is nothing wrong with parents having high expectations for their children, but they must be ready and willing to settle for the children's best. God holds them accountable for doing only their best with the gifts they have been given.

Family

The family is the very foundation upon which society rests. It is the first and often the only place where children are nurtured, loved and accepted for what they are, in an environment where they can learn principles and values that will help equip them for adulthood. Children can sense when family comes first and this will bring out the best in them. They thrive when parents exercise strong leadership; this tells them they are loved and thereby more receptive to instruction and guidance.

Children's minds are like sponges, absorbing whatever touches them. For better or worse, everything a child experiences in those formative years stays with them for the rest of their lives. Some people speculate that half of what people learn about living happens during the first six years of life. How difficult is it to remove stains from a sponge?

Parents are the first and most influential teachers their children will ever have. Informal learning takes place in the home through experience and example. "Train [instruct] your children in the way they should go, and when they are old [grown] they will not turn [stray] from it." (Proverbs 22:6) If they choose to do otherwise later in life, chances are they will return to the original, learned behavior. Whatever children learn in the home, RIGHT or WRONG, tends to remain with them throughout life. They will insist that whatever they learned is right even when it is wrong. It is very difficult for them (and us) to change.

Many modern cultural trends continue their devastating effect on the family: unhappy marriages, rising divorce rates, absent fathers, working mothers, the negative impact of increased television viewing, increased promiscuous sex, more single-parent households and unwed couples, violent crime up, tests scores down, increased use of drugs and alcohol, millions of school-age children home alone after school, increased depression and suicide, accessibility of pornography to younger children via the Internet, life without restraints, situational ethics replacing long-standing moral virtues, the need for and emphasis on immediate gratification — and the list goes on. Many kids are going off the deep end because their parents are not there to stop them or choose not to.

History is filled with great civilizations that have come and gone, all experiencing moral decay from within. Historian Edward Gibbon (1737-94) listed five major causes for the decline and fall of the Roman Empire:

- The rapid increase of divorce: the undermining of the dignity and sanctity of the home, which is the basis of human society.

- Increasingly higher taxes and the spending of public money for free bread and circuses for the populace.

- The mad craze for pleasure: sports becoming every year more exciting and more brutal.

- The building of gigantic armaments when the real enemy was within, the decadence of the people.

- The decay of religion—faith fading into mere form, losing touch with life and becoming less important to guide the people.

History does not document one civilization that survived without a dominating number of morally strong families. *How would you rate the moral state of America today?*

Parenting is one of the greatest challenges most adults will ever encounter. This is the first time in history that parents are no longer the main influence in child rearing; they must compete against the entertainment/advertising industry, television, Internet, research studies, and surveys. The amount of time, effort, and sacrifice (often unappreciated until later) required for children's physical, emotional, and spiritual needs (especially by mothers) are beyond one's imagination, unless you are a parent.

The opposite, however, is just as true. The parenthood experience is one of life's most gratifying and rewarding accomplishments. Nothing is more satisfying than seeing your grown children living independent, constructive and responsible lives. Animals leave their young only to get food and water and when their young are grown, they force them from the nest. Their job is done. No looking back. No guilt feelings. No regrets. Life moves on. In the human experience, the short-lived sacrifices parents need to make are more than worth the price.

Forgiveness

Forgiveness means to pardon; a matter of letting go of past incidents of resentment, anger and deep-seated hatred of others, and at times ourselves.

The medical profession informs us that these negative emotions are at the root of many of our physical ailments. "Unforgivingness" means being imprisoned by our past. Forgiveness frees us from floundering in that past.

When it comes to forgiving, there are those who seldom forgive. Then there are those who always forgive. That means the vast majority of us fall somewhere in between. Where do you appear on the continuum of forgiveness?

Most people tend to struggle with forgiving. We are more ready to be forgiven than to forgive. This attitude begins to change only when we begin to understand that forgiving benefits the forgiver as much or more than the forgiven.

Forgiveness is like exercising. When one begins to exercise, it may be painful and actually set one back. But the more one exercises, the better one's condition becomes. The better one's condition is, the more eagerly one will want to exercise. Once one begins to reap the benefits of forgiving, one will want to forgive more, not less.

How important is the topic of forgiveness? It is a recurring theme throughout Scripture; 125 separate references address it. A few examples follow:

"If you hold anything against anyone, forgive them."

"Forgive us our trespasses, as we forgive others."

"Forgive and you will be forgiven."

In the words of Miriam Stark: "Forgiveness is a gift that we choose to offer to those who have offended us. We give the gift; what they do with it is up to them. A true gift comes without expectations. Forgiveness allows us to live in peace with one another and with ourselves, which affords us the opportunity to step away from the hurt."

It also has been said, "Forgiveness is the sweetest revenge." What do you think?

Fruit of the Spirit

What is it? Spirit, according to the Bible, is God's presence that dwells in the mind of the believer and thereby generates certain "fruits" (blessings). The Fruits of the Spirit are love, joy, peace, patience, kindness, goodness, faithfulness, gentleness and self-control.

The Spirit of God gives birth to a new "heart" to live by.

1. **Love**—loving others the way God loves us.

   "Love is patient, love is kind. It does not envy, it does not boast, it is not proud. It is not rude, it is not self-seeking, it is not easily angered, it keeps no records of wrongs. Love does not delight in evil but rejoices with the truth. It always protects, always trusts, always hopes, always preserves. Love never fails."

   —1 Corinthians 13:4-8

2. **Joy**—knowing God is in control.

   "Possessing God's power enables us to face life with enthusiasm; it gives us a deep inward peace because we are not afraid of tomorrow. There comes into our lives an inner joy that outward circumstances cannot reach. Because God is within us, and because God is love, there flows out from us a love for others that sweeps away all prejudice, jealousy, and hate."

   —Charles L. Allen

3. **Peace**—resting serenely in the storms of life.

   "A soul divided against itself can never find peace. Peace cannot exist where there are contrary loyalties. For true peace there has to be psychological and moral harmony. Conscience must be at rest."

—Hubert van Zeller

4. **Patience**—overcoming our trials rather than have them overcome us.

   "Patience serves as a protection against wrongs as clothes do against cold. For if you put on more clothes, as the cold increases it will have no power to hurt you. So in like matter you must grow in patience when you meet with great wrongs, and they will then be powerless to vex your mind."

   —Leonardo da Vinci

5. **Kindness**—wanting the best for others.

   "Of all the things I have learned in my lifetime, the one with greatest value is that unexpected kindness is the most powerful, least costly, and most underrated agent of human change. Competition will improve quality and lower costs. Confidence will enable us to climb a mountain instead of a molehill. But kindness that catches us by surprise brings out the best in our natures."

   —Senator Bob Kerrey

6. **Goodness**—doing what is right.

   "The supreme test of goodness is not in the greater but in the smaller incidents of our character and practice; not what we are when standing in the searchlight of public scrutiny, but when we reach the firelight flicker of our homes; not what we are when some clarion-call wings through the air, summoning us to fight for life and liberty, but our attitude when we are called to sentry-duty in the grey morning, when the watch-fire is burning low. It is impossible to be our best at the supreme moment if character is corroded and eaten into by daily inconsistency, unfaithfulness, and besetting sin."

—F. B. Meyer

7. **Faithfulness**—unquestioning belief, trust and reliance on God.

"Faithfulness is not the shrugging of the shoulders or a passive posture. Nor is it a "grin and bear it" attitude. It is a positive, active attribute. It results from a love which keeps moving forward and comes out victorious. It remains steadfast and true in the midst of evil. The faithful person does not sidestep a situation or endeavor to escape to the easy path or flee when threats come. The faithful person stays at his station."

—John M. Drescher

8. **Gentleness**—being considerate of other people's shortcomings.

"There is no true and constant gentleness without humility. While we are so fond of ourselves, we are easily offended with others. Let us be persuaded that nothing is due to us, and then nothing will disturb us. Let us often think of our own infirmities, and we shall become indulgent towards those of others."

—Fenelon

9. **Self-control**—resisting temptations that are unacceptable to God.

Parents: "If a child is not disciplined and taught self-control early in the home, the grown-up world will take care of him later on, perhaps cruelly and when it is too late. A child curbed, taught obedience, spanked when he is young, rarely requires punishment when he hits his teens."

—John Warren Hill

The nine Fruits of the Spirit noted above and the many other virtues not listed here, all contribute to well-rounded, fruitful living.

Gifts That Last Forever

Caring

Cheerfulness

Encouragement

Forgiveness

Kindness

Listening

Love

Loyalty

Peacemaking

Praise

Prayer

Support

Time

Understanding

Giving

Giving, as opposed to possessing, means to hand over or part with something one owns to someone else. This could be one's time, talent, treasure or anything equally valued by most people.

Giving is something that doesn't come easily to most people. Human nature leans much more toward getting than giving. The attitude begins to change only when one begins to understand that giving benefits the giver even more than the receiver. "He who refreshes others will himself be refreshed."

When it comes to giving, most people always put themselves first. A few always put others first. All the rest of us fall somewhere in between. Where do you fall on the continuum of giving?

Formal giving of one's treasures goes back thousands of years to Old Testament biblical times. It was called tithing; it was in the form of a tax. "You shall truly tithe." It meant paying one-tenth of one's wealth to the church for religious functions.

Though not commanded in the New Testament, church members still view tithing as a guide for responsible financial giving. In fact, it encourages one to go even beyond tithing that reflects the believer's faith and love for God. This may also apply to one's time, talents, and more. "For where your treasure is, there your heart will be also."

Unfortunately, the vast majority of people view giving as an imposed-upon obligation rather than a privileged opportunity. For example, according to certain church officials, the average giving in most Protestant mainline denominations is two percent. They go on to say that members who give what they can, when they can, give an average of $460 per year. Those who pledge a specific amount of dollars each week give an average of $880 per year. Those who pledge a percentage of their income each week average $1,210 per year.

It's worth noting, for example, of those who tithe, seldom if ever does one stop once he or she starts. A few even give more. None gives less. When asked why, they say that they feel blessed, which supports the biblical passage: "It is more blessed to give than receive." One theologian is on record as saying, "This is the least believed verse in the Bible."

It has been stated that the best way to manage one's finances is to give ten percent, save ten percent, and learn to live on the remaining eighty percent. What do you think?

Giving is like exercising. When one begins to exercise, it may actually be painful and set one back; but the more one exercises, the better one's physical condition becomes. The better one's conditioning, the more likely one will want to exercise.

As soon as one begins to reap the benefits of exercise, one will want to exercise more, not less. So it is with giving. Once one begins to reap the mental and emotional benefits of giving, the tendency will be to give more and not less. "He who sows bountifully will reap bountifully. Give and it will be given to you.... For with the same measure that you use, it will be measured back to you."

God's F.L.A.G.

FAITH is having confidence, trust and dependence on something that cannot be proven, especially by reasoning.
"It is being sure of what we hope for and certain of what we do not see and without faith it is impossible to please God, because anyone who comes to Him must believe that He exists and that He rewards those who earnestly seek Him." Hebrew 11:1, 6.

Faith, then, is confidence in the absolute truthfulness of every statement, which comes from God. It requires complete unquestioning acceptance, especially something not supported by reason, even in the absence of proof.

Love is an active and positive response to the need(s) of another person(s).

"Love is patient, love is kind. It does not envy, it does not boast, it is not proud. It is not rude, it is not self-seeking, it is not easily angered, it keeps no record of wrongs. Love does not delight in evil but rejoices with the truth. It always protects, always trusts, always hopes, always perseveres. Love never fails." 1 Corinthians 13:4-8.

Jesus summed up the Ten Commandments in one word – LOVE. "Love God and love your neighbor [any person with whom you come in contact] as yourself." God promises that those who live by these words will be blessed and be a blessing to others.

Allegiance is a formal tie to that which one may choose to devote his or her loyalty. The focus here is God's laws as recorded in Scripture.

"If you fully obey the Lord your God and carefully follow all His commands I give you today, the Lord your God will set you [and your country] high above all the nations on earth. All these blessings will come upon you and accompany you if you obey the Lord your God: You will be blessed in the city and blessed in the country. You

will be blessed when you come in and blessed when you go out."
Deuteronomy 28: 1-3, 6.

Blessings are the product of obedience. Also, it needs to be noted
that the opposite is just as true.

Grace is the love and favor that God shows toward people even
though they do not deserve it. It frees us from our sinful nature. Our
good works, as important as they are, cannot do it alone. "For it is
by grace you have been saved, through faith, and this not from your-
selves, it is the gift of God not by works, so that no one can boast."

God's grace has the power to reclaim us from our sins and free
us from its bondage, making Salvation a reality. We are saved not by
what we do but by God's grace according to our faith. Thus, our
good works will be a reflection of God's grace at work in our lives.

As we continue on life's journey, may we focus on the virtues
stated above; they are consistent with Biblical teaching:

> **F**AITH to wear
> **L**OVE to care
> **A**LLEGIANCE to bear
> **G**RACE to share

May our attitude be one of gratitude for what we have, rather
than focus on what we don't have. May choosing to pledge allegiance to God's F.L.A.G. prove to be a blessing to you.

*This article evolved from gleaning a devotional that appeared in "Christ
in Our Home" by writer Anna Seden.*

Gossip

An unknown author had this to say on the subject: "My name is Gossip. I have no respect for justice; I ruin without killing; I tear down homes; I break hearts and wreck lives. I am wily, cunning, malicious, and I gather strength with age. I make my way where greed, mistrust, and dishonor are unknown. I feed on good and bad alike. My victims are as numerous as the sands of the sea, and often as innocent. I never forgive and seldom forget. My name is Gossip."

Man was created by God to live and work with his fellow man, not to hurt him; to build up, not tear down; to draw people together in love, not to separate them by strife.

If we catch in flight the impulse to be unkind and change it to a charitable word or action, we would make a big difference in the world. Isn't it worth the effort?

"Keep your tongue from evil, and your lips from speaking deceit."
—Psalm 34:13

Heredity and Environment

Children respond to their environment based to a great extent on their inherited characteristics. However, they should not be made to feel inferior or cheated because of hereditary differences. They have no control over it. They cannot change it. Their worth as a human being should not depend on it.

It is God's plan for them to be different; therefore, they should not be compared to one another. When parents view their children in this light, they not only prevent them from feeling inferior, but also they actually help them discover God's plan for their lives.

One of the most critical factors in children's lives is their environment. At the moment of conception, environment impacts on children physically, emotionally, and mentally. Since heredity is predetermined, there is little parents can do about it. But they can do a lot about the child's environment and this can make the biggest difference in how a child turns out. It is up to parents to provide a good environment for their children.

A healthy environment would include such things as the following:

- Providing safe conditions in which to grow up;

- Adapting discipline to the individual child;

- Spending as much time as possible with them;

- Correcting them in a loving way;

- Focusing on their strengths;

- Instilling a positive attitude;

- "Catching" them doing right;

- Helping them acquire a healthy self-image;

- Making children feel special;

- Supplying healthy physical and spiritual food.

Everything children experience in the environment is recorded in their minds—forever! The more caring the environment, the better children will respond and thrive.

Hope for America's Public Schools

There is not an urban district in America that can serve as a worthy example of quality public education in the modern age. What has happened?

The downward spiral in education began with the Supreme Court banned prayer in schools in 1962 and bible reading and reciting The Lord's Prayer in 1963. Until the 1960s religious acts not only were an integral part of public education in America, but also they had the blessing of our country's founders. Then in 1973 the Court legalized abortion. The trend continued with the banning of the schools' displays of the Ten Commandments (1980) and prayer at graduations (1992). Those Ten Commandments tell us how to love God and our neighbor and they have served society for thousands of years as a guide to help control violent outbursts and keep order in the world. When the Ten Commandments left the schools and when prayer ended, there was no moral code to replace them.

No one in our government is focusing on the real reason public schools are in such a mess. It is a moral problem and the Judicial Branch of our government helped create it. Nearly four decades of U.S. Supreme Court decision, propelled by the ACLU that banned biblical moral values from the classroom are producing children with amoral values. These decisions have led to the downfall of our public schools. Much behavior once considered abnormal has become the norm. Public education, as a result, has produced the following: low test scores, absenteeism, rampant violence, teen pregnancy, drug and alcohol addiction, abortion, unruly students roaming the halls, suicide, divorce, teachers being assaulted, gun violence and lack of respect for authority. The longer the moral issue is ignored, the greater the mess will become no matter how much money the government throws at it.

Responsible and frustrated parents are doing everything possible to rescue their children from the many government-owned, public schools that aren't getting the job done by sending them to private schools, and two million children are being home-schooled.

Although most parents tend to blame the schools when students don't do well, in reality the schools are simply a reflection of the homes from which the students come. They must accept the fact that it is they, and not the school, who are ultimately responsible for their children's education and they are the most important teachers their children will ever have. It is their example that will determine the attitude and behavior of their children.

To complicate matters even more, parents can't teach their children what they themselves don't know. If their own experiences were not good, their children's experiences won't be good and many of today's children have come from generations of scholastic and moral failures.

Because parents and schools play a significant part in the character development of children, it is important that they work together in presenting the character traits they wish to reinforce. This is made more difficult in light of the fact that parental involvement with the schools has slowly declined over the last 40 years.

While there is no short-term "easy-fix" to this "years-in-the-making" situation, the following is a small but feasible start at correcting one aspect. If every class has three or four students who are out of control, those few would account for a disproportionate share of the problems. These often life-threatening, chronic offenders stop others from learning and there seems to be no effective procedure in place to deal with them. Why not assign these individuals to a self-contained classroom all day taught by specially trained, higher paid teachers? They would remain there until they are ready to conduct themselves in a responsible manner. Even if they never learn or behave, for whatever reason, at least they wouldn't interfere with those students who want an education.

The message from our society is that there are no laws of morality that transcend us, everything is relative and that actions don't have consequences. As more and more people "do their own thing," right and wrong turn into relativism and absolutes become fewer and fewer. All are signs of a weakening moral climate. It is worthwhile to remember the words of General Douglas McArthur, "History fails to record a single precedent in which nations subject to moral decay have not passed into political and economic decline. There has been either a spiritual awakening to overcome the moral lapse or a progressive deterioration leading to ultimate national disaster."

The Public Boards of Education continue to spend more and more money on what hasn't worked. It's time to deal with the real problem—morality. Those who are in a position to do something about it are reluctant to confront it because it has religious implication, which makes it politically incorrect.

The answer to America's educational problems does not lie in more government spending, more laws, more police, or more jails, all of which at best put out fires rather than prevent them. We need to teach adults and children right from wrong and instill character traits, such as honesty, fairness, respect, honor, loyalty, kindness, dependability, and manners. The solution depends on a return to biblical moral values upon which our nation is founded.

PREKINDERGARTEN—THEN WHAT?

Government's response to a school problem often has been to throw more money at it (because it's politically correct, safe and easy) and then pretend there's progress. Not only does that action not rectify the problem, but also it has the potential to create bigger problems and often does.

The latest school movement in the government spotlight is "universal prekindergarten." Will this then be followed by more government-sponsored, preschool programs like *pre*-prekindergarten, day care, nursery school or infant care? In 300 years of education in America, government involvement has gone from zero participation to ninety-nine percent. Of course, prekindergarten and early childhood education (where tried) have had a positive influence, especially for those who would be fortunate enough to spend less time in a dysfunctional home environment. However, this is a short-lived, temporary benefit because it doesn't get to the root of the problem.

Education Policy Analyst Professor Diane Ravitch recently reported on various failed school reforms (academic, progressive, scientific, vocational) over the past hundred years which included curricular revision, IQ testing, new math, self-esteem, social adjustment, values clarification, school bussing and present-day charter schools. She stated, "Anything in education that is labeled a 'movement' should be avoided like the plague. To be effective, schools must concentrate on their fundamental mission of teaching and learning. And they must do it for all children. That must be the overarching goal of schools in the twenty-first century."

The solution to this particular social problem with its poverty-education correlation does not lie in more of the same government programs. George F. Wills of *The Washington Post* wrote, "Spending 6.6 trillion [much of which was misused] on poverty-related programs in four decades since President Johnson declared war on poverty is reason for concern. In fact, it has purchased a new paradigm of poverty."

One major noticeable change in our society in the 1950s was a weakening of the family and community. The public schools decided they must now do what the family and community used to do. Unfortunately, even at great expense to government, the schools lacked the capacity to take their place. It is time to confront and deal with the real challenge: educating those parents who need help so their children will be better equipped to benefit from what school has to offer and turn the tide by becoming better parents themselves. James Coleman, an education researcher, agrees: "The most important factor in how well a child achieves is not how much the school spends to teach him. Rather, the student's family background is the greatest determinant of performance."

Instead of prekindergarten, wouldn't it be wiser to apply that money, time and effort to family matters, such as marriage, parenting, children, youth and aging? Also, along with this, focus on extensive instruction on moral values. Parents must accept responsibility for how their children conduct themselves, because the values children learn before they go to school tend to remain with them.

PROBLEMS IN EDUCATION AREN'T ALL SCHOOL-RELATED. In a letter to a newspaper editor, teacher Louis Filippelli wrote the following: "The recent media revelations about the dismal state of the Cleveland public schools are refreshing in their truthfulness but frightening in their implications. The inner-city schools are a microcosm of a moral breakdown in urban areas that may be unprecedented in world history.

"The moral and social infrastructure of the central city may be crumbling past the point of no return. Multitudes within our inner-city communities have abandoned the value systems and societal norms of mainstream America and have embraced lifestyles that foster a renunciation and loathing of functional behavior in the family unit.

"The crisis facing Cleveland is a crisis of values. Most have abandoned the institution of marriage, and out-of-wedlock births are now the norm rather than the exception. Too many single mothers and absentee fathers have abdicated almost all traditional responsibilities and obligations and want to be accountable to no one.

"The schools must then deal with the emotionally and psychologically scarred children brought up in this cultural wasteland, where discipline and nurturing are conspicuously absent. Our schools are ill-equipped to deal effectively with the mass of humanity and its almost insurmountable array of social problems. The official response is to be politically correct and pretend we are making progress."

How Children Learn About Marriage

Children learn about marriage from their parents. This begins early in life. They use their parents' marriage as a model. This is what they take with them to their marriage and pass on to their children.

Children also need to be aware of the differences between husbands and wives. God created them male and female. God meant each to be unique. Though they differ physically, mentally and emotionally, they are all equal in His sight. The differing masculine and feminine gifts and talents are to be mutually respected and appreciated.

The Bible goes on to say that unless the Lord builds the house, they labor in vain who build it. Put another way, successful marriage is always a triangle: a man, a woman and God, and a cord of three strands is not quickly broken.

- Try to see the other's point of view.
- Resolve conflicts as soon as possible.
- Be as forgiving as possible.
- Ask what you can do to help.
- Try to maintain a prayerful attitude.
- Avoid blame. It only makes matters worse.
- Treat each other as you want to be treated.

Remember, it is important that you serve as a good role model for your children. They will be watching!

If I Were the Devil

I would gain control of the most powerful nation in the world;

I would delude their minds into thinking that they had come from man's effort, instead of God's blessings;

I would promote an attitude of loving things and using people, instead of the other way around;

I would dupe entire states into relying on gambling for their state revenue;

I would convince people that character is not an issue when it comes to leadership;

I would make it legal to take the life of unborn babies;

I would make it socially acceptable to take one's own life, and invent machines to make it convenient;

I would cheapen human life as much as possible so that the life of animals are valued more than human beings;

I would take God out of the schools, where even the mention of His name was grounds for a lawsuit;

I would come up with drugs that sedate the mind and target the young, and I would get sports heroes to advertise them;

I would get control of the media, so that every night I could pollute the mind of every family member for my agenda;

I would attack the family, the backbone of any nation;

I would make divorce acceptable and easy, even fashionable. If the family crumbles, so does the nation;

I would compel people to express their most depraved fantasies on canvas and movie screens, and I would call it art;

I would convince the world that people are born homosexuals, and that their lifestyles should be accepted and marveled;

I would convince the people that right and wrong are determined by a few who call themselves authorities and refer to their agenda as politically correct;

I would persuade people that the church is irrelevant and out of date, and the Bible is for the naïve;

I would dull the minds of Christians, and make them believe that prayer is not important, and that faithfulness and obedience are optional; I guess I would leave things pretty much the way they are.

—Paul Harvey

If Only

When was the last time you met someone who was truly content and at peace with the world? There are many such people! They usually got the wisdom to be that way by learning from the experiences of an active spiritual life. They discovered a sense of inner peace and contentment through their walk with God. But many folks eat their hearts out, suffering through the contagious "If Only" disease. Its germs infect every slice of life:

If only I had more money.

If only I could make better grades.

If only we owned a nicer home.

If only we hadn't made that bad investment.

If only I hadn't come from such a bad background.

If only she would have stayed married to me.

If only our pastor were a stronger preacher.

If only my child were able to walk.

If only we could have children.

If only we didn't have children.

If only the business could have succeeded.

If only my husband hadn't died so young.

If only I would've said "No" to drugs.

If only they had given me a break.

If only I hadn't had that accident.

If only we could get back on our feet.

If only he would ask me out.

If only people would accept me as I am.

If only my folks hadn't divorced.

If only I had more friends.

The list is endless. Woven through the fabric of all those words is an attitude that comes from the simple choice to see the negative side of life, the choice to be unhappy about almost everything that happens. Taken far enough, it leads to the dead-end street of self-pity—one of the most distasteful and inexcusable of all attitudes. Contentment, on the other hand, comes from another one of those simple choices, one that doesn't allow ourselves or others to listen to our list of woes. We simply choose to create a different kind of list—a positive one—for if we don't, people won't stay around us very long. Discontented souls soon become lonely souls.

—Charles Swindoll

It Must Have Been the Guns!

For the life of me, I can't understand what could have gone wrong in Littleton, Colorado. If only the parents had kept their children away from guns, we wouldn't have had such a tragedy. Yeah, it must have been the guns.

It couldn't have been because half of our children are being raised in broken homes. It couldn't have been because our children get to spend an average of thirty seconds in meaningful conversation with their parents each day. After all, we give our children quality time.

It couldn't have been because we treat our children as pets and our pets as children. It couldn't have been because we place our children in daycare centers where they learn their socialization skills among their peers under the law of the jungle, while employees who have no vested interest in the children look on and make sure that no blood is spilled.

It couldn't have been because we allow our children to watch, on average, seven hours of television a day filled with the glorification of sex and violence that isn't fit for adult consumption.

It couldn't have been because we allow our children to enter into virtual worlds in which, to win the game, one must kill as many opponents as possible in the most sadistic way possible.

It couldn't have been because we have sterilized and contracepted our families down to sizes so small, that the children we do have are so spoiled with material things that they come to equate the receiving of the material with love.

It couldn't have been because our children, who historically have been seen as a blessing from God, are now being viewed as either a mistake created when contraception fails or inconveniences that parents try to raise in their spare time.

It couldn't have been because our nation is the world leader in developing a culture of death in which 20 to 30 million babies have been killed by abortion. It couldn't have been because we give two-year sentences to teenagers who kill their newborns.

It couldn't have been because our school systems teach the children that they are nothing but glorified apes who have evolutionized out of some primordial soup of mud by teaching evolution as fact and by handing out condoms as if they were candy.

It couldn't have been because we teach our children that there are no laws of morality that transcend us, that everything is relative and that actions don't have consequences. What the heck, the President gets away with it. Nah, it must have been the guns.

—Addison L. Dawson

Just for Today

Just for today I will try to live through this day only, and not tackle my whole life problem at once. I can do something for twelve hours that would appall me if I felt that I had to keep it up for a lifetime.

Just for today I will be happy. This assumes to be true what Abraham Lincoln said, "Most folks are as happy as they make up their minds to be."

Just for today I will adjust myself to what is, and not try to adjust everything to my own desires. I will take my "luck" as it comes, and fit myself to it.

Just for today I will try to strengthen my mind. I will study. I will learn something useful. I will not be a mental loafer. I will read something that requires effort, thought and concentration.

Just for today I will exercise my soul in three ways: I will do somebody a good turn, and not get found out; if anybody knows of it, it will not count. I will do at least two things I don't want to do — just for exercise. I will not show anyone that my feelings are hurt; they may be hurt, but today I will not show it.

Just for today I will have a program. I may not follow it exactly, but I will have it. I will save myself from two pests: hurry and indecision.

Just for today I will have a quiet half hour all by myself, and relax. During this half hour, some time, I will try to get a better perspective of my life.

Just for today I will be unafraid. Especially I will not be afraid to enjoy what is beautiful, and to believe that as I give to the world, so the world will give to me.

Just for today I will be agreeable. I will look as well as I can, dress becomingly, talk low, be courteous, criticize not one bit, not find fault with anything and not try to improve or regulate anybody except myself.

—Alcoholics Anonymous (Revised)

Life's Journey

What determines which road you travel on your journey of life? What guidelines do you follow to navigate your own personal life and that of your children, and that influences how you conduct yourself with other people? What is your moral compass?

Everyone subscribes to someone, something or some kind of god or gods (philosophy) to determine what's right and what's wrong for them: academics, atheism, capitalism, communism, humanism, money, polytheism (many gods), power, popularity, narcissism, various religions, secularism, success and witchcraft, to name a few. What one serves is his or her "god."

Do you really know the right way to live? Our culture would have us believe that each individual is the ultimate authority of what's right and what's wrong, rather than following what has been proven to be right in the past. If someone you trust informs you that something is poisonous, for example, wouldn't it make sense to investigate it first before using it in some way?

Just as following natural laws protects us from physical harm, following moral laws shields us from much of life's needless suffering and permits us to live meaningful lives. People require and need sound standards to make good moral choices.

In order to achieve this, after a lifetime of contemplation, inquiry and comparison, my personal choice is The Holy Bible, specifically the Ten Commandments. These have proven to be the best way for me to determine right from wrong. In my opinion, they are applicable to everyone.

These laws need to be brought to the attention of as many people as possible, but not forced on anyone, except those involving murder, libel and theft. Situations require that each person thinks and decides which moral compass he or she chooses to follow and be prepared to live with the consequences. What a privilege it is to live in America where we have the freedom of choice.

Many argue that the Ten Commandments may have been applicable thousands of years ago but certainly not today. The truth is that these laws have provided wisdom through the ages and are as applicable today as they were when first given to Moses and the Nation of Israel thousands of years before Christ. They are at the very foundation of our moral code in determining right from wrong conduct.

James Madison said, "We have staked the whole future of American civilization not upon the power of government—far from it. We have staked the future of all of our political institutions upon the capacity of each and all of us to govern ourselves, to control ourselves, to sustain ourselves according to the Ten Commandments of God."

The Ten Commandments can be divided into two groups. The first four tell us how to love God. The remaining six tell us how to love and enhance our relationships with one another. God spoke these words saying:

1. **You shall have no other gods before me.** No deity real or imagined is to rival the one true God: not worshipping one's interest, time, talent, treasure.

2. **You shall not make for yourself an idol.** Do not worship false gods: carved images, sculptures, statues, pictures, culture and trends, because God is invisible and worshipped in spirit. An additional danger is that this example will be transmitted through parents, to their children and to those of future generations.

3. **You shall not take the name of the Lord your God in vain.** Do not curse, swear or show lack of reverence for the name of God.

4. **Remember the Sabbath day by keeping it holy.** "Six days you shall work, but the seventh day is a Sabbath to the Lord your God." It's a day of rest and spiritual rejuvenation. Also, this is a matter of exercising self-discipline. If people aren't content working six days, chances are they won't be content working seven.

5. **Honor your Father and your Mother.** Parents must teach their children to respect, honor and obey them. They can't and won't do it on their own. Parents need to realize that they represent God in their children's eyes and try their best to live lives worthy of their children's deepest respect and reverence. It is imperative that children be taught obedience to their parents.

6. **You shall not murder.** Do not inflict loss of life by illegal means. Jesus raised this commandment to a new level when he said, "You shall love your neighbor as yourself." When we fail to do this, we commit mental murder.

7. **You shall not commit adultery.** As a married person, do not commit acts of sexual unfaithfulness. Adultery "murders" a marriage. Fornication (sexual intercourse before marriage) is becoming epidemic among young people in today's society. Unfortunately, there is overt promotion by the culture of such behavior, enticing all to engage freely. This doesn't make it right.

Society is paying a terrible penalty for breaking these moral laws: divorce, children without love and guidance of both parents, abortion, unwanted children, sexual diseases, poverty, and more. Illicit sex before marriage is a wrong done to the future marriage and violates the commandment, just as adultery committed after marriage.

God's laws are always for our own good and the good of those around us. When not obeyed, negative consequences are not far behind, especially for those who believe we reap what we sow.

8. **You shall not steal.** Do not take anything without permission that doesn't belong to you. This includes such things as cheating, fraud, false advertising, dishonest labor, and not treating others the way you want to be treated.

9. **You shall not give false testimony against your neighbor.** Do not be disloyal toward another by distorting the truth with intent to deceive. A lie by any other name is still a lie: white lie, black lie, half-truth, distortion, deception. Many people think it's OK to lie as long as nobody knows about it. This is like falling and breaking a bone and telling others that it didn't happen. The bone is still broken.

10. **You shall not covet.** Do not feel envy (especially painful envy) for possessions or relationships that belong to others, to the point that they control you rather than the other way around. Since coveting is not illegal, people are free to choose. When desire and envy are not kept in check, they become our gods and supersede the God of the Bible. Those who take coveting to an extreme are seldom (if ever) satisfied.

The Ten Commandments are a combination of civil (legal) and moral laws. Commandments Six, Eight and Nine are civil laws enforced by the State. The other seven are moral laws followed by believers of the Bible but not enforced by the State. It doesn't make one category any less or more important than the other. This has become commonly known as "Separation of Church and State."

Jesus remained detached from politics (worldliness). "Render unto Caesar the things of Caesar and unto God [Godliness] the things of God." He was the first and only one to convey separation of Church and State and the United States became the first nation to actually practice it. History records that no other nation ever subscribed to separation of Church and State; they all left a trail of ruin, havoc, persecution, destruction and devastation.

Jesus summed up the Ten Commandments in one word — LOVE. When asked of all the commandments, which is the most important, he answered, "Love the Lord your God with all your heart and with all your soul and with all your mind and with all your strength. The second is this: Love your neighbor [any person with whom you come in contact] as yourself. There is no other commandment greater than these." (Mark 12:30-31)

God's promise is that those who live by these two commandments will be blessed and be a blessing to others. The choice is between Godliness and worldliness. "No one can serve two masters." It's like trying to go in two different directions at the same time—you end up going in circles and never reach your destination.

Listening

Effective listening is an important skill in communication and in developing and maintaining healthy interpersonal relationships.

Most of us are better at talking than listening. It takes desire and skill to hear, understand and remember what the other person is conveying to us. Body language is very important; it sometimes says what the person can't put into words. Other actions like tears, touching, hugs, eye contact and smiles communicate feelings, too.

Bridges in communication often vary with individuals: personal backgrounds that are similar, being in comfortable surroundings, having common interests, expressing similar ideas. Many times it's easier to communicate with someone of the same age. People who are good communicators know what they're talking about, are alert to their listener's responses and can put their message into concise words.

To be a good listener one must be patient and approachable. Allow others to have their own rights and feelings and try to see things from their point of view with an open mind. Use warm, friendly tones of voice. Politeness is basic to all human relations. Help others to find their own answers and solutions rather than providing easy ones for them.

Likewise, the blocks to effective communication can easily slip into the way if we let them. Being too busy or only listening with half an ear gives just part of our attention to what someone else is saying. Interruption, sarcasm, over-generalization and jumping to conclusions are other blocks that can stop the flow of conversation very quickly.

Effective listening requires a willingness to make an effort and invest a little of oneself in the process. It takes patience.

—*Senior Hotline*, Ohio State University Extension

Living the Moment

On what does your mind focus most of the time? When people are asked this question, the most frequent response is on the future, then the past, and lastly the present. This is unfortunate because the present is the most critical because that's where the action is.

Think about driving a car! Now and then we look back via the rear-view mirror. Occasionally, we look ahead to approaching areas. But mostly we need to focus on the immediate present in order to arrive safely at our destination. This illustration applies to living life as well.

Only after we begin to look back on our lives do we realize how much time, effort and worry we devoted to things, situations and circumstances that were and are out of our hands: little matters when we are young and bigger matters when we are older.

Any area of concern over which we have no control is cause for worry and becomes a "no win" situation that detracts us from where we can and do make a difference. Only after we begin to identify and dismiss those things that are out of our hands, are we in a position to focus our time and effort on the here-and-now in bringing about constructive and positive changes. This results in less worry, greater accomplishments and improved quality of life for the individual and those with whom he or she comes in contact.

Consider the following viewpoint. "First, I was dying to finish high school and start college. And then I was dying to finish college and start working. And then I was dying to marry and have children. And then I was dying for my children to grow old enough so I could return to work. And then I was dying to retire. And now, I am dying...and suddenly I realize I forgot to live."

There are two days in every week about which we should not worry—two days which should be kept free from fear and apprehension. One of those days is *yesterday*. Learn from its mistakes, faults, blunders, aches and pains, and put it away. The other day we should not worry about is *tomorrow* with its possible adversities, burdens and promises. This leaves only one day—*today*. Anyone can fight the battle of just one day. It is only when we add the burdens of yesterday and tomorrow that we break down.

In the words of writer Kay Lyon, "Yesterday is a cancelled check, tomorrow is a promissory note; today is the only cash we have—so spend it wisely."

Love

The word **love** means different things to different people. The Reverend Harry Wendt defines four different kinds of love. He writes the following:

The word "love" is sometimes confused with the word "like." Perhaps that is because the English language has only one word, "love," to explain a number of ideas. The Greek language, however, uses a number of terms:

Eros: Eros acts in response to an attraction in another person; it usually involves physical or sexual appeal. It is also an act of the emotions and cannot be commanded.

Philia: Has to do with companionship. It has often been called the "friendship" type of love.

Storge (store-gay): Refers to love between family members.

Agape (ah-gah-pay): This love acts in response to a need in another person. It is an act of the will, and *can* be commanded. This word is used to describe God's love for mankind, and the love people are to have for one another in response.

THE QUOTATIONS THAT FOLLOW FOCUS ON AGAPE LOVE:

Love is patient, love is kind. It does not envy, it does not boast, it is not proud. It is not rude, it is not self-seeking, it is not easily angered, it keeps no record of wrongs. Love does not delight in evil but rejoices with the truth. It always protects, always trusts, always hopes, always perseveres.

Love never fails. But where there are prophecies, they will cease; where there are tongues, they will be stilled; where there is knowledge, it will pass away. For we know in part and we prophesy in part, but when perfection comes, the imperfect disappears. When I was a child, I talked like a child, I thought like a child, I reasoned like a child. When I became a man [an adult], I put childish ways behind me. Now we see but a poor reflection as in a mirror; then we shall see face-to-face. Now I know in part; then I shall know fully, even as I am fully known. And now these three remain: faith, hope and love. But the greatest of these is love.

—1 Corinthians 13:4-13

We choose love by taking small steps of love every time there is an opportunity. A smile, a handshake, a word of encouragement, a phone call, a card, an embrace, a kind greeting, a gesture of support, a moment of attention, a helping hand, a present, a financial contribution, a visit—all these are little steps toward love.

—Henri J. M. Nouwen

Spread love everywhere you go: first of all in your own house. Give love to your children, to your wife or husband, to a next-door neighbor…. Let no one ever come to you without leaving better and happier. Be the living expression of God's kindness; kindness in your face, kindness in your eyes, kindness in your smile, kindness in your warm greeting.

—Mother Teresa

God's love is unconditional and people, especially children, need unconditional love. They need to be loved if they are to grow up to be loving. They need love, security, and acceptance from the very beginning. They need praise, encouragement, and instruction more than correction, even when they are not very loving.

—Daniel Taddeo

So loving my enemies does not apparently mean thinking them nice either. That is an enormous relief. For a good many people imagine forgiving your enemies means making out that they are really not such bad fellows after all, when it is quite plain that they are.

—C. S. Lewis

Managing Stress

Stress is the reaction of our bodies and minds to anything that upsets their regular balance.

Accept yourself as you are. Don't try to be someone you aren't.

Accustom yourself to unreasonableness and injustice. Unfairness is common around us.

Allow more time to get where you're going. It usually takes longer.

Always look on the positive side. It's the most constructive thing to do.

Be prepared to wait in line. Cultivate patience.

Concern yourself with the present. Tomorrow will take care of itself.

Deal with the little problems. It prevents big ones.

Discipline your children. Everyone will benefit from it.

Do the most important things first. And do them one at a time.

Exercise often. It does even more good than most people realize.

Expect four out of five traffic lights to be red. Devote the time to prayer and introspection.

Focus on things as they are rather than how you want them to be.

Get outside of yourself. Help lighten the burdens of others.

Live within your means. Do everything possible to stay out of debt.

Schedule fewer activities. This allows time for the unforeseen.

Take care of yourself. That includes a balanced diet and eight hours of sleep.

View trying circumstances as character-building opportunities. This results in the greatest good.

Watch less TV, especially "news" programs. TV is out to promote its own agenda.

We are not responsible for the actions of others. We can only change ourselves.

Write things down. Stop trying to remember everything.

It's our perception of a situation that's at the root of much of the stress in our lives, more than the actual circumstances. It's important for people to learn what they can do when confronted with stressful events, because too much stress will cause physical and emotional damage.

Marriage

Children learn about marriage from their parents. This begins very early in life. They use their parents' marriage as a model. This is what they take with them to their marriage and pass on to their children. They should be exposed to the struggles as well as the successes. Their expectations need to be realistic. Somehow the message that marriage is not all fun and games doesn't get through. They need to know that all households have their share of sadness and joy. Parents should not hesitate to discuss these matters at the appropriate time. Many opportunities to do this will arise naturally, such as at mealtimes, weddings, funerals, reunions and hundreds of other occasions. Discussing the Christian marriage with children helps prepare them for the event in their own lives.

In the beginning God established the marriage bond. "'…Have you not read that He who made them at the beginning made them male and female.' And said, 'For this reason a man shall leave his father and mother and be joined to his wife, and the two shall become one flesh.' " Marriage is the most intimate relationship; and it was designed to be one of the most fulfilling and rewarding. For this to be true, however, biblical principles pertaining to marriage must be followed. "Unless the Lord builds the house, they labor in vain who build it…." Marriage is not a human invention; it is God's creation.

For marriage to be what God intended, He has to be at the center. My way and your way are replaced with His way: looking upward rather than inward. "Submitting to one another in the fear [reverence] of God." Mutually submitting to one another and to God means husbands and wives are able to consider the needs of the other as more important than their own. To do this they keep God at the center of their marriage and submit to His teachings. When their fragile support lines intertwine with Him, they form an unbreakable cord. "And a threefold cord is not quickly broken." Since all husbands and wives are imperfect, they should not expect perfection in their marriage. Only God is perfect. This is why with God at the center of the marriage, all things become manageable.

One of the most important factors in marriage is choosing the right partner. The Bible is very specific about this. "Do not be unequally yoked together with unbelievers...." This means the marriage will be built using two different sets of blueprints. Being equally yoked means using the same set of blueprints to build the marriage. Neither will be built without hard work. But which one is likely to encounter more problems? The most important ingredient of a good and happy Christian marriage is that husband and wife share a common faith and belief in God. Though this doesn't guarantee a good marriage, couples who do not share a common faith are more likely to experience difficulties in marriage. Children need to be made aware of this information even though they may choose to ignore it when they select their marriage partner.

Children also need to be aware of the differences between husbands and wives. God meant each of them to be unique. Though they differ physically, mentally, emotionally, and may have different gifts, they are all of equal value and importance in God's eyes. God didn't put all strengths of character in one sex. The differing masculine and feminine gifts and talents are to be mutually respected and appreciated. They are intended to complement, not battle against each other. This understanding is not only essential for a good marriage, but also it provides a solid sex identity model for healthy childrearing by doing such things as the following: trying to see the other's point of view; resolving conflicts as soon as possible; being as forgiving as possible; asking what he or she can do to help; trying to maintain a prayerful attitude; learning to be the person God wants him or her to be; avoiding blame because it only makes matters worse; and treating each other as he or she would want to be treated.

Remember, it's important that you serve as a good role model for your children. They'll be watching!

Morality

The Colorado school shooting will continue to be with us. The void it left in the lives of those directly affected by the tragedy is known only to them. The grieving process will last for years—for some, a lifetime.

There's much speculation about possible causes: culture violence, inattentive parents, video games, the Internet and lax gun laws, to mention a few.

The Clinton administration was all for spending more to beef up security, increase police officers and pass more gun control laws. Many see this as taking the easy way out. It's more of what hasn't worked because it doesn't get to the root of the problem. You can't prevent fires by simply buying more fire trucks. I think this is a moral problem.

Consider the latest changes in our society today. They have been listed in our ten-year census from 1960 to 2000. They include dramatic increases in crime, drug and alcohol addiction, epidemic violence, illegitimate births, abortion, child abuse, single-parent homes, juvenile arrests and drop in test scores. There's every indication that the near future census will reveal even more.

As more and more people "do their own thing," right and wrong turn into relativism and absolutes become fewer and fewer. Both are signs of a weakening moral climate.

Douglas MacArthur reminds us that, "History fails to record a single precedent in which nations subject to moral decay have not passed into political and economic decline. There has been either a spiritual awakening to overcome the moral lapse, or a progressive deterioration leading to ultimate national disaster."

My first year of teaching was 1956. Each school day began with the Pledge of Allegiance, selected Bible reading, personal application and prayer. The emphasis was on God, family, country and citizenship.

Typical school problems at that time were gum chewing, excessive talking, running in the halls and some improper dress. Thirty-five years later, drug and alcohol addiction, rampant violence, teen pregnancies and assaults became common.

What brought about these changes? One, the Supreme Court handed down some earth-shaking decisions. The Bible, prayer and the Ten Commandments were outlawed from school. Two, teachers could no longer teach moral values. God was driven from the classroom.

It wasn't long before character erosion set in. Character traits, such as honesty, fairness, respect, honor, loyalty, kindness, dependability and manners began to deteriorate. Part of the thinking was, since there's lack of agreement on which moral values to teach, "We won't teach any!"

Moral values must be an active force in the lives of everyone. When this is not the case, people will get hurt. Every person is affected by the actions of others in some way, at some time, and in some place.

One sure way to help instill moral values in children is found in Proverbs 22:6, "Train a child in the way he should go and when he is old, he will not turn from it." Parents must do this very early. When children get big, it's too late.

Rearing children was never meant to be as complicated as many have made it. Parents need to rely less on books and experts (who often omit God from the equation) and more on life's instruction manual—the Bible and their own common sense.

Instructing children is best done by example. This is the most dominant force in child development. Parents also need help from other parents and vice versa. It's almost impossible to do it alone, because parents can't always be with their children.

The solution, in my opinion, to rid our nation of its ills is found in II Chronicles 7:14, "If my people who are called by my name will humble themselves, and pray and seek my face, and turn from their wicked ways, then I will hear from heaven, and will forgive their sin and *heal* their land."

It's obvious to most people that a moral society is much preferred over an immoral one. For this to happen, people need to have loving hearts and be willing to place their faith and trust in God, not politics.

New Year's Resolutions

Let this coming year be better than all the others. Vow to do some of the things you've always wanted to do, but couldn't find the time.

Call up a forgotten friend. Drop an old grudge and replace it with some pleasant memories. Share a funny story with someone whose spirits are dragging. A good laugh can be very good medicine.

Vow not to make a promise you don't think you can keep. Pay a debt. Give a soft answer. Free yourself of envy and malice. Encourage some youth to do his or her best. Share your experiences and offer support. Young people need role models.

Make a genuine effort to stay in closer touch with family and good friends. Resolve to stop magnifying small problems and shooting from the lip. Words you have to eat can be hard to digest.

Find time to be kind and thoughtful. All of us have the same allotment: 24 hours a day. Give a compliment. It might give someone a badly needed lift.

Think things through. Forgive an injustice. Listen more. Be kind.

Apologize when you realize you are wrong. An apology never diminishes a person. It elevates him. Don't blow your own horn. If you've done something praiseworthy, someone will notice eventually.

Try to understand a point of view that is different from your own. Few things are 100 percent one way or another. Examine the demands you make on others.

Lighten up. When you feel like blowing your top, ask yourself, "Will it matter a week from today?" Laugh the loudest when the joke is on you.

The sure way to have a friend is to be one. We are all connected by our humanity, and we need each other. Avoid malcontents and pessimists. They drag you down and contribute nothing.

Don't discourage a beginner from trying something risky. Nothing ventured means nothing gained. Be optimistic. The can-do spirit is the fuel that makes things go.

Go to war against animosity and complacency. Express your gratitude. Give credit when it's due—even when it isn't. It will make you look good.

Read something uplifting. Deep-six the trash. You wouldn't eat garbage. Why put it in your head? Don't abandon your old-fashioned principles. They never go out of style. When courage is needed, ask yourself, "If not me, who? If not now, when?"

Take better care of yourself. Pass up that second helping. You really don't need it. Vow to eat more sensibly. You'll feel better and look better, too. And you'll weigh less, and wouldn't that be nice?

Don't put up with second-hand smoke. Nobody has the right to pollute your air or give you cancer. If someone says, "This is a free country," remind him or her that the country may be free, but no person is free if he has a habit he can't control.

Return those books you borrowed. Reschedule that missed dental appointment. Clean out your closet. Take those photos out of the drawer and put them in an album. If you see litter on the sidewalk, pick it up instead of walking over it.

Give yourself a reality check. Phoniness is transparent and tiresome. Take pleasure in the beauty and the wonders of nature. A flower is God's miracle.

Walk tall and smile more. You'll look ten years younger. Don't be afraid to say, "I love you." Say it again. They are the sweetest words in the world. If you have love in your life, consider yourself blessed, and vow to make this the best year ever.

—Ann Landers

Notable Quotables

A man falls in love through his eyes, a woman through her ears.
—Woodrow Wyatt

A thankful heart is not only the greatest virtue, but the parent of all other virtues.—Cicero

All virtue is loving right, all sin is loving wrong.
—Hubert Van Zeller

Be wiser than other people if you can, but do not tell them.
—Lord Chesterfield

Courage is going from failure to failure without losing enthusiasm.
—Winston Churchill

Delight in the success of others; it benefits everybody.
—Daniel Taddeo

Do not bite the bait of pleasure till you know there is no hook beneath it.—Thomas Jefferson

Either the Bible will keep us away from sin, or sin will keep us away from the Bible.—C. S. Lewis

Hating people is like burning your own house down to get rid of a rat.—Harry Emerson Fosdick

He who conceals his sins does not prosper, but whoever confesses and renounces them finds mercy.—Epictetus

If a thing is worth doing, it's worth doing well.—Lord Chesterfield

If you really want insight about yourself, ask someone you know, trust and respect.—Daniel Taddeo

If you want to lift yourself up, lift up someone else.
—Booker T. Washington

Is prayer your steering wheel or your spare tire?
—Carrie Ten Boom

It is easy to dodge our responsibilities but we cannot dodge the consequences…—Josiah Charles Stamp

It is far easier to be wise for others than to be so for oneself.
—Francois de La Rochefoucauld

Learn to unlearn and then relearn.—Daniel Taddeo

Men are not punished for their sins, but by them.
—Elbert Hubbard

No act of kindness, no matter how small, is ever wasted.—Aesop

No one can make you feel inferior without your consent.
—Eleanor Roosevelt

One should examine oneself for a very long time before thinking of condemning others.—Moliere

Part of our problem with debt is that we have confused needs with wants.—Billy Graham

People who love wealth are seldom satisfied with their income.
—Ecclesiastes 3:10

Say only those things about people that you would say if they were present.—Daniel Taddeo

The gem cannot be polished without friction, nor man perfected without trials.—Confucius

The larger the island of knowledge, the longer the shoreline of wonder.—Ralph W. Sockman

The way to get things done is not to mind who gets the credit.
—Benjamin Jowett

The weak can never forgive. Forgiveness is an attribute of the strong.—Mahatma Gandhi

Things turn out best for the people who make the best of the way things turn out.—John Wooden

Thinking isn't agreeing or disagreeing. That's voting.
—Robert Frost

This is the day the Lord has made; let us rejoice and be glad in it.
—Psalm 118:24

We always weaken whatever we exaggerate.
—Jean-Francois de La Harpe

We are masters of the unsaid words, but slaves of those we let slip out.—Winston Churchill

We do not see things as they are. We see things as we are.
—The Talmud

We have all failed to practice ourselves the kind of behavior we expect from other people.—C. S. Lewis

Worry is like a rocking chair: it gives you something to do but never gets you anywhere.—Erma Bombeck

You can give without loving, but you cannot love without giving.—Amy Carmichael

You can't hold a man down without staying down with him. —Booker T. Washington

You catch more flies with honey than with vinegar. —Henry IV of France

Zeal is fit only for wise people, but it is found mostly in fools. —Thomas Fuller

Obedience

O bedience is the key to successful parenting and it must begin early. We're told that children recognize their mother's voice while still in the womb. It should come as no surprise that children are capable of manipulating their parents long before they learn to walk or talk.

Some think children learn half of what they will ever know before school age; and it remains with them the rest of their lives. Unless children learn to respect and obey their parents, they will not respect and obey their teachers, their employers or the law.

Parents need to keep family life simple, especially during the early years. Don't explain every little thing. Children have no reasoning ability at this age. They only know what they think they want when they want it. Fear is the most effective way to communicate with this age group.

Because children are so different, parents need to learn their unique traits and discipline them accordingly. This means spending a lot of time getting to know them. What works with one may not work with another. Parents talk too much and act too little. Mean what you say or don't say it. Always follow through. Do whatever it takes to get children to obey, including spanking as a last resort.

Parents have the authority and responsibility to raise law-abiding children. They need to be aware that their children view them as God (all knowing) on whom they're totally dependent, mostly they want to please and be accepted and they tend to respond better to a positive approach and normal tone of voice. Parents who scream and yell the most usually have children who obey the least.

Parents who really love their children do not overlook or accept excuses for their inappropriate behavior. Yet, it happens all the time. Why would parents allow their two-year-old to defy them when they know it's wrong? Not only is this destructive, but also it teaches children that they know more than their parents.

Children should do what they're told. They may have input but no final say so on what's really important. There's plenty of time for this later. Children first have to learn right from wrong and to obey. Disobedient children feel confused, frustrated and unloved. They're miserable and they make others miserable.

It's sad how afraid many parents are of their children's temporary disappointments and unhappiness. Parents should not feel they're doing something wrong or feel guilty when they say "NO" to their children. This is probably exactly what they need. Children need to adapt to parents and not the other way around. This isn't to say parents won't make mistakes. But then, children don't need nor do they expect perfect parents.

Instilling obedience in children is one of the more important and challenging responsibilities of parenting.

On This Day

Mend a quarrel.
Seek out a forgotten friend.
Write a love letter.
Share a treasure.
Encourage a young person.
Keep a promise.
Find the time.
Count your blessings.
Forego a grudge.
Forgive someone.
Listen.
Give a soft answer.
Apologize if you were wrong.
Try to understand that certain person.
Examine your demands on someone.
Appreciate.
Express your gratitude.
Be kind.
Be gentle.
Laugh a little more.
Show enthusiasm all day.
Welcome a stranger.
Gladden the heart of a child.
Take pleasure in the beauty and wonder of the earth.
Speak your love. Speak it again. Speak it still again.

—Author Unknown

Out of Our Hands

Only after we begin to look back on our lives, do we realize how much time, effort, and worry we devote to things, situations, and circumstances that are out of our hands.

During our earlier years we often focus on such things as where we live, our personal appearance, and trying to be something other than ourselves. During the later years the load becomes heavier and heavier with such things as will our team win, our personal health, divorce, crime, cancer, AIDS, terrorism, the economy, and the threat of war and death, to name a few.

Any area of concern that we have no control over is cause for worry and becomes a "no win" situation. Only after we begin to identify and dismiss those things that are out of our hands, are we in a position to focus out time and effort toward helping to bring about positive change. This results in less worry, greater accomplishments and improved quality of life.

Paradox of Our Time

The paradox of our time in history is that we have taller buildings, but shorter tempers; wider freeways, but narrower viewpoints; we spend more, but have less; we buy more, but enjoy it less.

We have bigger houses and small families; more conveniences, but less time; we have more degrees, but less sense; more knowledge, but less judgment; more experts, but more problems; more medicine, but less wellness.

We drink too much, smoke too much, spend too much, laugh too little, drive too fast, get angry too quickly, stay up too late, get up too tired, read too seldom, watch TV too much, and pray too seldom.

We have multiplied our possessions, but reduced our values. We talk too much, love too seldom, and hate too often. We've learned how to make a living, but not a life; we've added years to our life, not life to years.

We've been all the way to the moon and back, but have trouble crossing the street to meet the new neighbor. We've conquered outer space, but not inner space. We've done larger things, but not better things.

We've cleaned up the air, but polluted the soul. We've split the atom, but not our prejudice. We write more, but learn less; we plan more, but accomplish less.

We've learned to rush, but not to wait; we have higher incomes, but lower morals; we have more food, but less appeasement; we build more computers to hold more information to produce more copies than ever, but have less communication; we've become long on quantity, but short on quality.

These are the times of fast foods and slow digestion; tall men, and short characters; steep profits, and shallow relationships. These are the times of world peace, but domestic warfare; more leisure, but less fun; more kinds of food, but less nutrition.

These are the days of two incomes, but more divorce and of fancier houses, but broken homes. These are the days of quick trips, disposable diapers, throw-away morality, one-night stands, overweight bodies, and pills that do everything from cheer to quiet, to kill.

It is a time when there is much in the show window and nothing in the stockroom; a time when technology can bring a letter to you, and a time when you can choose either to make a difference, or just hit delete.

—Author Unknown (Conflicting Origin)

Picks from Proverbs

The fear of the Lord is the beginning of knowledge, but fools despise wisdom and discipline.

Do not withhold good from those who deserve it, when it is in your power to act.

Whoever loves discipline loves knowledge, but he who hates correction is stupid.

The plans of the righteous are just, but the advice of the wicked is deceitful.

The Lord detests lying lips, but he delights in men who are truthful.

He who walks with the wise grows wise, but a companion of fools suffers harm.

Misfortune pursues the sinner, but prosperity is the reward of the righteous.

He who spares the rod hates his son, but he who loves him is careful to discipline him.

He whose walk is upright fears the Lord, but he whose ways are devious despises him.

There is a way that seems right to a man, but in the end it leads to death.

A simple man believes anything, but a prudent man gives thought to his steps.

A gentle answer turns away wrath, but a harsh word stirs up anger.

He who ignores discipline despises himself, but whoever heeds correction gains understanding.

Better a little with righteousness than much gain with injustice.

If a man pays back evil for good, evil will never leave his house.

Starting a quarrel is like breaching a dam; so drop the matter before a dispute breaks out.

Even a fool is thought wise if he keeps silent, and discerning if he holds his tongue.

Food gained by fraud tastes sweet to a man, but he ends up with a mouth full of gravel.

The glory of young men is their strength, gray hair the splendor of the old.

Train a child in the way he should go, and when he is old he will not turn from it.

The rich rule over the poor, and the borrower is servant to the lender.

Do not withhold discipline from a child; if you punish him with the rod, he will not die.

Do not envy wicked men; do not desire their company.

Do not say, "I'll do to him as he has done to me; I'll pay that man back for what he did."

A word aptly spoken is like apples of gold in settings of silver.

Seldom set foot in your neighbor's house—too much of you, and he will hate you.

If your enemy is hungry, give him food to eat; if he is thirsty, give him water to drink.

Do not answer a fool according to his folly, or you will be like him yourself.

Like one who seizes a dog by the ears is a passer-by who meddles in a quarrel not his own.

Do not boast about tomorrow, for you do not know what a day may bring forth.

Let another praise you, and not your own mouth; someone else, and not your own lips.

Better is open rebuke than hidden love.

Better a poor man whose walk is blameless than a rich man whose ways are perverse.

He who conceals his sins does not prosper, but whoever confesses and renounces them finds mercy.

He who rebukes a man will in the end gain more favor than he who has a flattering tongue.

A fool gives full vent to his anger, but a wise man keeps himself under control.

Where there is no revelation, the people cast off restraint; but blessed is he who keeps the law.

Practice the Apology

Once you realize you don't have to make yourself wrong to deliver an apology, you'll feel a new power. If you differ strongly with a friend on a political matter, you can say the following: "My passion for my own beliefs has made it difficult to fully understand yours. If it has caused trouble between us, I apologize. My relationship with you is far more important than whether we agree or not."

And if you have a strained situation with your boss and feel misunderstood, at least you can say, "I'm sorry for the tension that has developed between us. I intend to find a way to work it out."

If your teenage daughter screams at you that you are ruining her life with your rules, you can say, "My rules are meant to protect you and teach you how to get along with people. I'm sorry for any bossiness or coldness that I may have delivered with my message."

We cannot always act in perfect harmony with the people we love. They inevitably will feel upset, misunderstood and frustrated by things we do. But we don't have to get so caught up with figuring out who is right and who is wrong that we forget what matters. "Because of deep love, we are courageous," said the Chinese philosopher Lao-Tse more than 2,000 years ago. The power of an apology is a tool to affirm the primacy of our connection with others. It can unlock deep love in our everyday lives. Don't wait. Apologize!

—Rosamund Stone Zander, Psychotherapist

Prayer

Perhaps nothing on the subject of prayer has ever been uttered more wisely than the following speech in the Constitutional Convention of 1787. The speaker was in his 82nd year:

> In the beginning of the contest with Britain, when we were sensible of danger, we had daily prayers in this room for the Divine Protection. Our prayers, Sir, were heard, and they were graciously answered. All of us who were engaged in the struggle must have observed frequent instances of a Superintending providence in our favor. To that kind providence we owe this happy opportunity of consulting in peace on the means of establishing our future national felicity.

> And have we now forgotten this powerful Friend? Or do we imagine we no longer need His assistance. I have lived for a long time; and the longer I live, the more convincing proofs I see of this truth—that God governs in the affairs of men. And if a sparrow cannot fall to the ground without His notice, is it probably that an empire can rise without his aid?

> We have been assured, Sir, in the Sacred Writings, that "Except the Lord build the house, they labor in vain that build it." I firmly believe this; and I also believe that without His concurring aid we shall proceed in this political building no better than the builders of Babel: we shall be divided by our little, partial, local interests; our prospects will be confounded; and we ourselves shall become a reproach and a by-word down to future ages.

And what is worse, mankind may hereafter from this unfortunate instance, despair of establishing government by human wisdom, and leave it to chance, war, or conquest. I therefore beg leave to move that henceforth prayers, imploring the assistance of Heaven and its blessing on our deliberations, be held in this assembly every morning before we proceed to business; and that one or more of the clergy of this city be requested to officiate in that service.

—Benjamin Franklin

Principles of Parenting

Love abundantly. This gives children a sense of security, belonging and support. Parental love should be constant and unconditional. It should also be open and expressed often. Parents should hug and praise their children at every available opportunity.

Discipline constructively. Discipline means setting and adhering to standards of behavior. It helps the child adjust to the outside world and makes him better behaved and happier. Discipline should be consistent, clear and reasonable.

Spend time together. Time should be spent playing with the children, talking together (listening and reacting to one another), teaching and with family activities. "You can't fool children by giving them things rather than your time and attention."

Tend to personal and marital needs. To relate well to children, parents must be comfortable with themselves. By treating yourself well, you'll avoid the feeling of being mistreated, used unfairly, or overburdened when something goes wrong. A household in which love is openly expressed is a household in which children flourish. Verbalizing love to one's children is not enough. Parents should make every effort to let their youngsters see warmth and tenderness in their marital relationship.

Teach right from wrong. Children need to be taught basic values and manners in order for them to get along well in society. Parents should clearly state their own moral values and discuss them with their children.

Develop mutual respect. All family members should treat each other with respect. That means parents should act in respectful ways to their children, too. "Thank you," "Excuse me," "I'm sorry" are not just for kids. If parents treat each other with respect and love, and teach children to respect their parents, a solid foundation will be laid.

Really listen. Parents should really listen to their child, from his or her earliest years. That means giving undivided attention, putting aside one's own thoughts and beliefs and trying to understand the child's point of view. It also means encouraging the expression of feelings—both good and bad—and allowing the child to show hostility or anger without fear of losing your love.

Offer guidance. But, be brief. Don't make a speech. And encourage the child to think about the problem and come up with possible solutions himself.

Foster independence. Gradually allow children more and more freedom or control over their own lives. But as one parent said, "Once your children are old enough, kind of phase yourself out of the picture. But always be near when they need you."

Be realistic. Expect your child to make mistakes. Realize that outside influences, like peer pressure, increases as children mature.

—Author Unknown

Priorities

Spiritual: "You shall love the Lord your God with all your heart, with all your soul, and with all your strength."

Family: "Choose for yourself this day whom you will serve…but as for me and my house, we will serve the Lord."

Neighbors: "You shall love your neighbor as yourself."

Health: "Do you not know that your body is the temple of the Holy Spirit who is in you, whom you have from God, and you are not your own?"

Work: "And whatever you do, do it heartily, as to the Lord and not to men."

Education: "You shall teach them [God's Laws"] diligently to your children, and shall talk of them when you sit in your house, when you walk by the way, when you lie down, and when you rise up."

Money: "For the love of money is a root of all kinds of evil."

Material Comforts: "Seek the kingdom of God, and all these things shall be added to you."

Quotes to Ponder

WORDS OF WISDOM

1. You cannot legislate the poor into prosperity by legislating the wealthy out of prosperity.

2. What one person receives without working for, another person must work for without receiving.

3. The government cannot give to anybody anything that the government does not first take from somebody else.

4. When half of the people get the idea that they do not have to work because the other half is going to take care of them, and when the other half gets the idea that it does no good to work, because somebody else is going to get what they work for, that my dear friend, is the beginning of the end of any nation.

5. You cannot multiply wealth by dividing it.

LIFE IS A FOUR-SIDED AFFAIR.

"Life is a four-sided affair. Your daring program is going to lead you into physical [health] adventures, mental [wisdom] adventures, social [relationships] adventures, spiritual [Godly] adventures. You have not one, but four lives to live – a four-fold opportunity to grow. …It is helping you touch life at all angles, absorb strength from all contacts, pour out power on all fronts. The more you pour out, the more you find to pour."

—William H. Danforth (1870-1956)

PRIORITIES

"I am not bound to win but I am bound to be true. I am not bound to succeed but I am bound to live up to what light I have. I must stand with anybody that stands right; stand with him while he is right and part with him when he goes wrong."

—Abraham Lincoln

FORGIVENESS

"Everyone has the capacity to forgive; and everyone owes it to himself to do so at every turn in life. Research shows that people who make a habit of forgiving may have lower blood pressure, a stronger immune system, less susceptibility to heart attack, and the upper hand on a number of health issues. They are happier and able to think more clearly. They have unburdened themselves from the weight of anger and freed themselves to go about their lives."

—Edward M. Hallowell, M.D.

WHERE IS YOUR TREASURE?

"For where your treasure is, there your heart will be also."

—Luke 12:34

PRAYER FOR SERENITY

"O God, grant us the serenity to accept what cannot be changed; the courage to change what can be changed; and the wisdom to know the one from the other."

—Reinhold Niebuhr

THINGS YOU CAN'T RECOVER

The stone, after the throw.
The word, after it's said.
The occasion, after it's missed.
The time, after it's gone.

FREEDOM

"In the end, more than freedom, they [ancient Athens] wanted security. They wanted a comfortable life, and they lost it all – security, comfort, and freedom. When the Athenians finally wanted not to give to society but for society to give to them, when the freedom they wished for most was freedom from responsibility, then Athens ceased to be free and was never free again."

—Edward Gibbon, historian

HAPPINESS
Forgive.
Apologize.
Admit errors.
Listen to advice.
Keep your temper.
Shoulder the blame.
Make the best of things.
Maintain high standards.
Think first before you act.
Think first before you speak.
Put the needs of others before your own.
Leave every place you've been a little better.

FOUR THINGS
"Four things a man must learn to do
if he would make his record true:

To think without confusion clearly;
To love his fellow man sincerely;
To act from honest motives purely;
To trust in God and Heaven securely."

—Henry Van Dyke

NEVER DOUBT

"…that a small group of thoughtful, committed citizens can change the world. Indeed, it's the only thing that ever has."

—Margaret Mead

STAND FOR SOMETHING

"Stand for something. Don't quest for popularity at the expense of morality and ethics and honesty. Daniel Webster taught this country that what is popular is not always right, and what is right is not always popular."

—Howard Cosell

SHORT COURSE IN GOOD RELATIONS

The six most important words: I admit that I was wrong.
The five most important words: You did a good job.
The four most important words: What do you think?
The three most important words: Could you please?
The two most important words: Thank you.
The most important word: We.
And the least important word: I.

Reconciliation

One of the things I had to work through was the relationship I had with my father. He wasn't the kind of father who played catch with me or took me to ballgames. He didn't come to my games to watch me. He wasn't one to give hugs or say he loved me. He wasn't one to ever praise me if I did something good but he sure let me know if he thought I did something wrong. In brief, he wasn't the father I wanted him to be and I resented him for it.

When he died I had to reconcile these feelings of resentment with a very unexpected (on my part) deep feeling of loss! Why did I feel this emptiness—this void in my life over someone whom I resented? As I meditated on this, I began to think about my father in the context of who he was, not who he wasn't! He was a father who saw to it that I was fed well, had good clothes and a roof over my head. He and my mother stayed married (58 years) and provided family stability in my life. He taught me good old-fashioned German pride and discipline. (Boy, do those Germans know about discipline!) He took me into the secure and stable future. And, although it was never said, I guess I knew deep down that if I ever had a serious problem, or got into trouble, I could go to him for help.

No, my father wasn't Robert Young from "Father Knows Best"— he wasn't a buddy, a pal, or ever a very good friend. But, in his own way, he did the best he could and that is all we can ask of anybody. In retrospect, I now realize how fortunate I was to have him as my father! I now realize why I feel such a deep loss!

The reason I have shared this with you is because I now realize that when my father was alive I looked for his faults—and found them. After his death, I looked for his good points—and I found them! It dawned on me that the quality of our relationships with one another comes down to what we look for in each other. If we look for the bad—that is what we will find. Conversely, if we look for the good in a person, we will find that, too!

Unfortunately, I think many of our relationships suffer because we spend the majority of time looking for the bad in one another. I wonder what the world (Rwanda, Bosnia-Serbia, England-Ireland, the list goes on and on) would be like if people made a concentrated effort to look for the good in others instead of the bad. As a matter of fact, how would our personal lives be different if we did this with friends, relatives and even (or especially) with members of the church community?

Well, realistically there probably isn't too much you and I can do about the world problems. But what we can do is work on our relationships with the people in our daily lives. We can make a better effort at looking for the good in people and not the bad. Maybe another way of expressing what I am trying to say is: "Let there be peace on earth, and let it begin with me!"

—Gary Kronenberger

Relationships

Relationships are connections between people, places, and things and how they relate to one another. They can be voluntary or involuntary, positive or negative, constructive or destructive.

There are good relationships but no perfect ones because there are no perfect people. The challenge is to nurture the best relationships possible with family members, friends andcoworkers.

I want to focus here on people relationships that are voluntary, positive and constructive. What are the ingredients of such relationships? What follows is my attempt to answer this question.

Six guiding principles in establishing healthy relationships appear in the Bible in the fourth chapter of Philippians, where we are encouraged to meditate on any virtue and anything praiseworthy, including the following: whatever things are **true** (accurate, factual, genuine); **noble** (honorable, sincere, trustworthy); **just** (honest, impartial, lawful); **pure** (moral, sinless, uncorrupted); **lovely** (enjoyable, loving, pleasing); and **of good report** (beneficial, prudent, suitable).

Avoiding the negative aspects of conduct is a great enhancement to building meaningful relationships. In Ephesians 4:31-32 we read: "Let all bitterness, wrath, anger, clamor, and evil speaking be put away from you, with all malice. And be kind to one another, tenderhearted, forgiving one another, even as God in Christ forgave you."

Should we not adhere to this instruction, we not only hurt ourselves and others, but also we displease God.

As important as it is to have a loving relationship with people, it is even more critical that every individual experience a personal relationship with the God of Scripture. Better to have a personal relationship with Him than to attend church and not have it. Of course, having it and attending church would be even more beneficial.

Cultivating voluntary, positive, constructive personal relationships helps make the impossible possible. Life is all about relationships.

Rules of Civility

Every action in company ought to be with some sign of respect to those present.

Speak not when others speak, sit not when others stand, and walk not when others stop.

When a man does all he can, though it succeeds not well, blame not him that did it.

Think before you speak; pronounce not imperfectly, nor bring out your words too hastily, but orderly and distinctly.

Be not curious to know the affairs of others, neither approach to those that speak in private.

Undertake not what you cannot perform; but be careful to keep your promise.

Speak no evil of the absent, for it is unjust.

Associate yourself with men of good quality if you esteem your own reputation, for it is better to be alone than in bad company.

Speak not injurious words, neither in jest or earnest. Scoff at none, although they give occasion.

Go not thither where you know not whether you shall be welcome or not. Give not advice without being asked; and when desired, do it briefly.

—George Washington
(1732-1799)

Self-Esteem

Parents can help their children build a healthy sense of self in the following specific ways:

- Set healthy boundaries for your child and be consistent in enforcing them.

- Give your child opportunities to make as many choices as possible (i.e., offer them two choices that you can live with, letting them make the final decision for themselves). This gives your child the opportunity to practice decision-making skills and tells them that you trust them to make their own choices. What an encouragement!

- Do not rescue your child from their consequences. You are doing your child a grave disservice when you teach them that bad choices do not reap consequences.

- Let your children experience disappointments. It is important for children to learn that they will not always be the best and that's okay. Empathize with their disappointment but remind them that doing their best and having a good character are the most important. (By the way, parents, you have to believe this, too!)

- Praise your children in specific ways, focusing on the good choices they make.

- Instead of lecturing your child, try to empathize with how they are feeling and talk with them about how they might handle the situation differently next time. Then end with a statement of confidence in their ability to make good choices. Failure to make a good choice does not mean that they cannot do better next time.

- Encourage your child not to back down from difficulties in life. For example, if your child got a 55% on a math test, hold back the lecture and try asking them to tell you about a problem they got right on the test. This encourages them to share their failure with you and gives you the opportunity to show them that they are capable despite their recent failure. You will encourage them to keep trying by finding hope in a grim situation.

- These are just a few of the many ways that we can work to build our children's self-confidence. Our goal should be to empower our children to build confidence in their ability "of being capable of meeting life's challenges and being worthy of happiness," not to facilitate it for them.

—Bridgette Tempner, Home and School Counselor

Sin

Sin is an offense against the *moral* laws of God, distinguished from vice and crime in *legal* or ethical sense. Traditionally, the most familiar offenses are the original Seven Deadly Sins described by Thomas Aquinas (1225-74):

1. Pride (excessive belief in one's own worth)
2. Covetousness (greed)
3. Lust (excessive craving of affection)
4. Anger (madness rage)
5. Gluttony (desire to overeat)
6. Envy (bitter resentfulness)
7. Sloth (laziness)

Other lists include crime, cruelty, adultery, selfishness, bigotry, dishonesty, and hypocrisy as other worst "sins" and, of course, there are more.

In his book *Whatever Became of Sin?*, Dr. Karl Menninger, a well-known psychiatrist, states that the word *sin* has almost completely disappeared from our vocabulary because our perception of evil has changed. Deviant behavior is no longer considered sin, but an illness to be dealt with scientifically. Nevertheless, sin by any other name is still sin.

Sin is very real and its power to condemn is deadly. The main problem of the human race, world wide, is sin. One of the main reasons for this is that we compromise in not labeling sin for what it is.

Just as responsible conduct, such as kindness, goodness, respectability, honesty, ethical conduct, trustworthiness, morality and respectability (the opposite of sinful behavior) produces positive results, irresponsible conduct (sin by whatever the name) generates negative consequences. They might not surface immediately, but over a lifetime the results invariably will prove to be negative in one way or another.

Consider the three following simple illustrations: provide proper maintenance for your car and have dependable transportation; supply your body with good food, exercise, and rest and enjoy good health; treat others the way you want to be treated, and all stand to benefit.

When it comes to personal conduct and behavior, everyone has the freedom to choose one of two roads for life's journey: the popular, self-centered road or the less popular, God-centered road. As recorded in the Bible's third chapter of Timothy 2, those who choose the self-centered road will be more inclined to "…be lovers of themselves, lovers of money, boastful, proud, abusive, disobedient to their parents, ungrateful, unholy, without love, unforgiving, slanderous, without self-control, brutal, not lovers of the good, treacherous, rash, conceited, lovers of pleasure rather than lovers of God—having a form of godliness but denying its power…."

Those who choose the God-centered road will be much more inclined to treat others the way they would want to be treated. God-centered conduct minimizes or even prevents sin; whereas, self-centered conduct maximizes or even guarantees sin, confirming the fact that we reap what we sow.

Six Benefits of Consistent Exercise

Being faithful to your work routine can be tough, but the results you will get are well worth the effort. Toning and losing weight are only part of an exercise program's benefits. Consider the following:

Relax better. Leisure activity will be more meaningful since you are feeling better about your body.

Reduce your stress level. You will be more alert at work and better able to tackle new challenges.

Build your self-confidence. Not only will looking better increase your self-respect, but also exercising will improve your mental outlook.

Improve your concentration. Breaking everyday routine with exercise is one of the best ways to get a fresh start.

Increase your creativity. Exercise increases the flow of oxygen, giving new energy. Tired minds become refreshed.

Stop worry. Whether it is money, job or something else, exercise clears the mind and slows down worry.

Working out gives you more than a better-looking body. It changes the way you see yourself and everything around you.

—*The Journal of the American Medical Association*

Standing Against the Tide

Abraham Lincoln, sixteenth President of these United States, is everlasting in the memory of this country. For on the battleground of Gettysburg, this is what he said: "The occasion is piled high with difficulty, and we must rise with the occasion. We must disenthrall ourselves and then we shall save our country."

At that time slavery divided and threatened our country. Some 150 years later the unraveling of the family and undermining of our moral foundations has become that threat. What Lincoln said then applies equally today. The occasion "piled high with difficulty" is the eternal struggle between two principles: right and wrong. We must rebuild the foundation of our country by restoring, renewing, and strengthening the moral values upon which it was founded – "and then we shall save our country."

Why have special interest groups and organizations like the ACLU and Americans United for the Separation of Church and Sate, who represent only a small minority of Americans, been so successful at constantly seeking ways to remove religion from both our private and public lives by subtly twisting the First Amendment? For the answer in part we need to look at our voting record. In the words of Edmund Burke, "The only thing necessary for the triumph of evil is for good men to do nothing."

Over half of all eligible voters in America don't vote for governors, members of Congress, or Presidential candidates.

[Edward Everett Hale said, "I am only one, but I am one. I cannot do everything, but I can do something. What I can do, I should do and, with the help of God, I will do!"]

—Matt Finneran

Success

Success: What is it? Webster defines it as the result that was hoped for: the fact of becoming rich, famous, etc. Generally speaking, success falls in either one of two categories: *Godly*, the God-centered way of love toward God and love toward others, and *worldly*, the self-centered way of greed and unconcern for the welfare of others. We are required to make choices, like it or not. We can't have it both ways.

Most people who seek success choose the becoming rich and famous route. Theologian Herbert W. Armstrong writes about just such people: "Their definition of success was material acquisition, recognition of status by society, and the passing enjoyment of the five senses. But the more they acquired, the more they wanted, and the less satisfied they became with what they had. When they got it, it was never enough." A prime example of this is King Solomon, called the wisest and wealthiest man who ever lived. He had it all and concluded at the end of his life, "It was all vain—a striving after wind."

"Why are only the very few—women as well as men—successful in life?" asks Armstrong. "Just what is success? Here is the surprising answer to life's most difficult problem, proving that no human need ever become a failure! All who have succeeded have followed these seven laws of success:

"1. **Fix the right goal.** The very first law of success is to be able to define success! Once you have learned what success is, make that your goal in life.

"2. **Education, or preparation.** We have to learn, to study, to be educated, to be prepared for what we propose to do. Right education must not stop at teaching TO LIVE! It must know, and teach, the purpose of human life, and how to fulfill it.

"3. **Health.** We are physical beings and are just what we eat. Of course there are other laws of health: sufficient sleep, exercise, plenty of fresh air, cleanliness and proper elimination, right thinking, clean living.

"4. **Drive.** Half-hearted effort might carry one a little way toward his goal, but it will never get him far enough to reach it. Without energy, drive, constant propulsion, a person need never expect to become truly successful.

"5. **Resourcefulness.** When complications, obstacles, unexpected circumstances appear to block your path, you must be equipped with RESOURCEFULNESS to solve the problem, overcome the obstacle, and continue on your course.

"6. **Perseverance, stick-to-it-iveness.** Nine in ten, at least once or twice in a lifetime, come to the place where they appear to be totally defeated! All is lost—apparently, that is. They give up and quit, when just a little more determined hanging on, just a little more faith and perseverance, just a little more stick-to-it-iveness would have turned apparent certain failure into glorious success.

"7. **God.** This all-important Law of Success is having contact with, and the guidance and continuous help of God. And the person who does put it last is very probably dooming his life to failure at the end.

"The only way to success is not a copyrighted formula being sold for a price. You can't buy it! The price is your own application to the seven existing laws."

What do *you* think? Do you agree? Do you disagree?

Teenage Suicides

The many suicides of our youth is tragic and a blight on our nation. They cause many broken hearts and homes. These are some of the reasons given by young people, particularly teenagers, why they think there are so many suicides: Nobody cares about them; their parents don't know they're alive; they hate themselves; they don't fit in with others unkind to them; they're not attractive enough; their peers ignore them or ridicule them; they are in trouble and they think there's no way out; their troubles will never end and there's no hope for their future.

They are influenced by others to do it, and mentally abused by step-fathers, live-in boyfriends, relatives, even priests, ministers, school teachers and scout leaders. What a sick world! Many children are yelled at and beaten by parents who are alcohol and/or drug addicts.

There is no love, no peace in their homes, only fear, loneliness, hurt, rejection and hopelessness. Most of them lack what many of us take for granted. They don't eat well, sleep well or have clean clothes. Rich or poor, they all need love, time spent with them, interest in what they say or do, and lots of prayer.

They do a lot of foolish things just to get anybody's attention. Is it any wonder why we have the world's largest prison population, mostly young men and women, too? Why we have so many teen pregnancies, alcoholics? The immorality, lack of common sense, traditional and moral values, alternative lifestyles, brings much confusion to their minds and emotions.

Then, there are also added hurts, rejection and anger that build up because of divorce and constant aggravation in their families. These are often the result of pressures, anxiety and weariness when both parents have to work and still keep up with the maintenance of the home.

When I was a youngster, before TV came on the scene, boys played with marbles, played baseball, went skating, rode bikes, played pitched cards, went fishing and exploring, did some chores to help out and kept busy. Girls, also, were busy in many varieties of activities, learning to cook, playing games and learning about babies, playing with dolls, etc.

Mothers were usually at home with the children. Families did things together. They went to church, ate together, took car rides, visited neighbors, relatives and friends, went on picnics. Families don't do many things together anymore today (generally speaking). Too many are going their separate ways, no time left for each other.

We learned character, morality and honesty at home, at school and at our churches and synagogues. My, how times have changed! Some things very good and some very bad! Life goes on and there are always changes. Other generations have said these same words.

"Good families" and dysfunctional families are both facing these problems with their children today. Rebellion is in their hearts. Lawyers, judges, pastors, psychologists just don't have the answers, neither does the government. Money can't fix the problem; there isn't enough money in the world to fix it.

—Don Dembs

Television

Television is one of the greatest inventions of all time. Since the 1950s it has affected people's lives more than any other technological development. For the first time in history, something other than parents has become the main provider of information, values and entertainment for children. TV has changed how the family functions, how people think, what they buy, how they dress, and what they do during their free time.

Surveys tell us that average pre-school-age children, age two to five, spend a third or more of their total waking hours watching TV. Most children will spend more time watching TV than any other single activity during the first 18 years of their lives except sleep.

Television can be a great blessing. At its best it can inform, expand and enrich the lives of adults and children; but it can also be a curse. It can rob adults and children of their moral and spiritual values and cripple their mental, emotional and physical development. The wrong use of television can do the following: cause confusion between right and wrong; retard social development; make learning in school more difficult; shorten attention span; reduce attentiveness; discourage self-discipline; harm parent-child relationships; interfere with mealtime; increase boredom; promote spectatorship rather than participation; rob time from reading, writing, conversing, playing, exercising and imagining; and mislead children into believing difficult problems can be easily solved in a short period of time.

Parents are responsible for preventing television from ruling their family. They should not assume that TV is always acceptable entertainment. In fact, the opposite is true. TV programming is saturated with violence, sex, distorted role models, trivia and immorality. In addition to all of the above and more, TV viewing is extremely passive. Children put little into it; therefore, they get little value out of it. Plus, they've wasted valuable time that could be put to better use.

Parents should be very selective about which programs they allow their children to view, including the nightly "news" programs. The emphasis on violence and dramatic footage can be very disturbing and destructive. The mass media is a major force in forming our attitudes of right and wrong. Most television writers and producers are convinced that focus on the "forbidden fruit" will increase the demand for their product because they think that's what the viewing public wants. As a result, broadcasting guidelines are pushed to the limit in downgrading language, moral values, good taste, speech, dress, manners, respect, kindness, and concern for others.

Often the programs are so captivating that even Christians fail to change channels or turn off the TV. The Bible says, "Do not be conformed to this world, but be transformed by the renewing of your mind, that you may prove what is that good and acceptable and perfect will of God." God's word should serve as the final authority on what we should accept or reject from the broadcasting industry.

According to the American Academy of Pediatrics, children should be limited to watching no more than two hours of TV a day. It helps to decide ahead of time which programs to watch. Having only one TV in the home will help achieve this goal.

The time gained can then be spent on more constructive activities. They could include such things as reading, using the library, listening to good radio programming, playing games, conversing with friends and family members, taking trips, learning to get along with others and many other activities where children are actively involved gaining life-lasting skills and benefits.

Ten Commandments for a Successful Marriage

1. Put your mate before your mother, your father, your son and your daughter, for your mate is your lifelong companion.

2. Do not abuse your body with excessive food, tobacco or drink, so that your life may be long and healthy, in the presence of those you love.

3. Do not permit your business or your hobby to make you a stranger to your children, for the most precious gift a parent can give his or her family is time.

4. Do not forget that cleanliness is a virtue.

5. Do not make your mate a beggar, but willingly share with him or her your worldly goods.

6. Remember to say, "I love you." For even though your love may be constant, your mate yearns to hear those words.

7. Remember always that the approval of your mate is worth more than the admiring glances of a hundred strangers, so remain faithful and loyal to your mate, and forsake all others.

8. Keep your home in good repair, for out of it will come the joys of old age.

9. Forgive with grace. For who among us does not need to be forgiven?

10. Honor the Lord your God all the days of your life, and your children will grow up and bless you.

—Abigail Van Buren

The Educated Man

Whom do I call educated? First, those who manage well the circumstances which they encounter day by day and those who possess a judgment which is accurate in meeting occasions as they arise and rarely miss the expedient course of action.

Next, those who are decent and honorable in their intercourse with all men, bearing easily and good-naturedly what is unpleasant and offensive to others, and being as agreeable and reasonable to their associates as it is humanly possible to be.

Furthermore, those who hold their pleasures always under control and are not ultimately overcome by their misfortunes, bearing up under them bravely and in a manner worthy of our common nature.

Finally, and most important of all, those who are not spoiled by their successes, who do not desert their true selves, but hold their ground steadfastly as wise and sober-minded men, rejoicing no more in the good things that have come to them through chance than in those which, through their own nature and intelligence, are theirs since birth.

Those who have a character which is in accord, not with one of these things, but with all of them—these I maintain are educated and whole men possessed of all the virtues of a man.

—Socrates
(468-399 B.C.)

The Hand I Was Dealt!

When you hear people say, "This is the hand I was dealt," it usually refers to some negative event that happens in their lives. Consider instead the mental and physical powers that God has given you. Develop this even further and compare this to a deck of playing cards. There are four suits: spades, clubs, hearts and diamonds. You can use these as symbols when you apply the aforementioned powers that God has given you.

The first power can be symbolized by **SPADES**. You have been given the ability to dig, to investigate, and to search for treasures in many fields of endeavor. The most productive field in which to dig is Holy Scripture, especially the Bible. In John 5:39 we read, "You diligently study the Scriptures because you think that by them, you possess eternal life." This is a true testimonial to the fact that the death and resurrection of Christ assures us of eternal life.

In your hand, you also hold **CLUBS**. The club can be used to strike down evil that arises in your heart. You can even use words and deeds to attack evil. In Jeremiah 23:29 we read, "Is not my word like fire?" declares the Lord, "And like a hammer that breaks a rock in pieces?" Also in Jeremiah 18:18 we read, "Come let's attack him with our tongues."

The hand you hold also contains **DIAMONDS**. Of infinite value are spiritual diamonds, the most precious of which is faith, a diamond of inestimable worth, for it gets you into heaven. St. Peter in I Peter 3:3-4 speaks of spiritual diamonds as adornments far superior to "gold, jewelry and fine clothes," namely, "the unfading beauty of a gentle and quiet spirit, which is of great worth in God's sight." The life of a Christian sparkles with the diamonds of truthfulness, sincerity, honesty and honor.

Then, there are **HEARTS**. Among God's gifts to you is not only the heart pulsating in your breast, but also the inner self, which abounds with love, compassion and courage. Most people, I believe, think more of this inner self than the physical heart. You have a heart enabling you to go on amid life's difficulties, a heart to show your love to others, and for Christians a heart you have given to God in response to His great love to you.

So, in your hand you hold spades, clubs, diamonds and hearts. Use them in God's glory. Our prayer should be to ask God to help you to make greater use of the personal gifts and powers He has given you.

—Dallas Queck, Church Deacon

The Importance of Here and Now

In our culture, all of us are preoccupied most of the time with anticipating the future and worrying about it or with daydreaming about the past and remembering how it was. We are always trying to be happier right now, and yet much of what we do prevents us from achieving that happiness.

To be in the here and now means to be in touch with our senses, to be aware of what we are seeing, hearing, smelling, and so on. Young children find it very easy to be in the here and now; if we watch them play, we will notice that they seldom worry about what is going to happen an hour or two hours from now, and that they spend little time reminiscing. They are concerned with the present situation and with getting the most from it.

If, as teenagers and adults, we could be more like young children, many of the problems that bother us would disappear.

Think about how many nights we were not able to get to sleep because we were thinking about the future or the past; how many hours of the day we wasted and how many opportunities we have missed by not allowing our mind and body to experience what is happening now. There is a saying, "The future is only a dream and the past no longer exists. The present moment is the only reality."

The Lord's Prayer

Prayer is an acknowledgment of our dependence upon God. It is the communion of the people of God with their heavenly Father. Prayer consists of praise, thanksgiving and confession. God's people present their prayers to God and leave it to Him to decide whether it is wise to grant the requests or not. God alone knows whether the content of the prayer would be for their own good or for the good of God's kingdom.

One day Jesus was praying in a certain place. When He finished, one of His disciples said to Him, "Lord, teach us to pray." Jesus responded with His teaching on prayer, which people later called **The Lord's Prayer**. He told them to pray the following:

Our Father in heaven, hallowed be Your name. Just as very young children are totally dependent on their parents for survival, people of all ages stand to benefit from a similar relationship with their heavenly Father.

Your kingdom come. Your will be done on earth as it is in heaven. This refers to the heavenly, spiritual Kingdom of God to be established on earth at Christ's Second Coming to rule over all nations in the name of Love.

Give us this day our daily bread. Bread represents the necessities of life, not the luxuries—our needs, not our wants. Montaigne wrote, "We are not to pray that all things may go on as we would have them, but as most conducing to the good of the world."

And forgive us our debts, as we forgive our debtors. There is a connection between the first and the second part of this petition. If you forgive others, you will be forgiven. We reap what we sow.

And do not lead us into temptation, but deliver us from the evil one. The request is for God's help in avoiding the array of worldly temptations. It will not be easy.

For Yours is the kingdom and the power and the glory forever. This refers to the Heavenly Kingdom of God that will be established on earth when Christ returns to rule over all nations with love, peace, joy and justice for all.

Amen. So be it.

"Our Father in heaven, hallowed be Your name. Your kingdom come. Your will be done on earth as it is in heaven. Give us this day our daily bread. And forgive us our debts, as we forgive our debtors. And do not lead us into temptation, but deliver us from the evil one. For Yours is the kingdom and the power and the glory forever. Amen."

The sixty-six words in this model prayer, as recorded in the sixth chapter of Matthew, serve as a guide for one's own personal prayer time.

The Optimist's Creed

To be so strong that nothing can disturb your peace of mind.

To talk health, happiness and prosperity to every person you meet.

To make all your friends feel that there is something in them.

To look at the sunny side of everything and make your optimism come true.

To think only of the best, to work only for the best, and to expect only the best.

To be just as enthusiastic about the success of others as you are about your own.

To forget the mistakes of the past and press on to the greater achievements of the future.

To wear a cheerful countenance at all times and give every living creature you meet a smile.

To give so much time to the improvement of yourself that you have no time to criticize others.

To be too large for worry, too noble for anger, too strong for fear, and too happy to permit the presence of trouble.

—Author Unknown

The Rocks in Your Life

A philosophy professor stood before his class and had some items in front of him. When class began, wordlessly he picked up a large, empty mayonnaise jar and proceeded to fill it with rocks, rocks about two inches in diameter. He then asked the students if the jar was full. They agreed it was.

So the professor then picked up a box of pebbles and poured them into the jar. He shook the jar lightly. The pebbles, of course, rolled into the open areas between the rocks. He then asked the students if the jar was full. They agreed it was.

The students laughed. The professor picked up a box of sand and poured it into the jar. Of course, the sand filled up everything else.

"Now," said the professor, "I want you to recognize that this is your life. The rocks are the important things, your family, your partner, your health, your children—anything that is so important to you that if it were lost, you would be nearly destroyed. The pebbles are the other things that matter like your job, your house, your car. The sand is everything else—the small stuff.

"If you put the sand into the jar first, there is no room for the pebbles or the rocks. The same goes for your life. If you spend all your energy and time on the small stuff, you will never have room for the things that are critical to your happiness. Play with your children. Take time to get medical checkups. Take your partner out dancing.

"There will always be time to go to work, clean the house, give a dinner party and fix the disposal. Take care of the rocks first—the things that really matter. Set your priorities. The rest is just sand."

—Author Unknown

The Room

In that place between wakefulness and dreams, I found myself in
the room. There were no distinguishing features save for one wall
covered with small index card files. They were like the ones in librar-
ies that list titles by author or subject in alphabetical order. But these
files, which stretched from floor to ceiling and seemingly endlessly
in either direction, had very different headings.

As I drew near the wall of files, the first to catch my attention
was one that read "People I Have Liked." I opened it and began flip-
ping through the cards.

I quickly shut it, shocked to realize that I recognized the names
written on each one.

And then without being told, I knew exactly where I was. This
lifeless room with its small files was a crude catalog system for my
life. Here were written the actions of my every moment, big and
small, in a detail my memory couldn't match.

A sense of wonder and curiosity, coupled with horror, stirred
within me as I began randomly opening files and exploring their
content. Some brought joy and sweet memories; others a sense of
shame and regret so intense that I would look over my shoulder to
see if anyone was watching. A file named "Friends" was next to one
marked "Friends I Have Betrayed."

The titles ranged from the mundane to the outright weird. "Books
I Have Read," "Lies I Have Told," "Comfort I Have Given," "Jokes
I Have Laughed At." Some were almost hilarious in their exact-
ness: "Things I've Yelled at My Brothers." Others I couldn't laugh
at: "Things I have Done in My Anger." "Things I have Muttered
Under My Breath at My Parents." I never ceased to be surprised by
the contents. Often there were many more cards than I expected.
Sometimes fewer than I hoped.

I was overwhelmed by the sheer volume of the life I had lived. Could it be possible that I had the time in my short life to write each of these thousands or even millions of cards? But each card confirmed this truth. Each was written in my own handwriting. Each signed with my own signature.

When I came to a file marked "Lustful Thoughts," I felt a chill run through my body. I pulled the file out only an inch, not willing to test its size, and drew out a card. I shuddered at its detailed content. I felt sick to think that such a moment had been recorded.

An almost animal rage broke on me. One thought dominated my mind: No one must ever see these cards! No one must ever see this room! I have to destroy them. In an insane frenzy I yanked the file out. Its size didn't matter now. I had to empty it and burn the cards.

But as I took it at one end and began pounding it on the floor, I could not dislodge a single card. I became desperate and pulled out a card, only to find it as strong as steel when I tried to tear it.

Defeated and utterly helpless, I returned the file to its slot. Leaning my forehead against the wall, I let out a long, self-pitying sigh. And then I saw it. The title bore "People I have Shared the Gospel With." The handle was brighter than those around it, newer, almost unused. I pulled on its handle and a small box not more than 3 inches long fell into my hands. I could count the cards it contained on one hand.

And then the tears came. I began to weep. Sobs so deep that the hurt started in my stomach and shook through me. I fell on my knees and cried. I cried out of shame from the overwhelming shame of it all. The rows of file shelves swirled in my tear-filled eyes. No one must ever, ever know of this room. I must lock it up and hide the key.

But then as I pushed away the tears, I saw Him. No, please not Him. Not here. Oh, anyone but Jesus. I watched helplessly as He began to open the files and read the cards. I couldn't bear to watch His response. And in the moments I could bring myself to look at His face, I saw a sorrow deeper than my own. He seemed to intuitively go to the worst boxes. Why did He have to read every one?

Finally He turned and looked at me from across the room. He looked at me with pity in His eyes. But this was a pity that didn't anger me. I dropped my head, covered my face with my hands and began to cry again. He walked over and put His arm around me. He could have said so many things. But He didn't say a word. He just cried with me.

Then He got up and walked back to the wall of files. Starting at one end of the room, He took out a file and, one by one, began to sign His name over mine on each card.

"No!" I shouted rushing to Him. All I could find to say was "No, no," as I pulled the card from Him. His name shouldn't be on these cards. But there it was, written in red so rich, so dark, so alive. The name of Jesus covered mine. It was written with His blood.

He gently took the card back. He smiled a sad smile and began to sign the cards. I don't think I'll ever understand how He did it so quickly, but the next instant it seemed I heard Him close the last file and walk back to my side. He placed His hand on my shoulder and said, "It is finished."

I stood up, and He led me out of the room. There was no lock on its door. There were still cards to be written.

—Author Unknown

The Value of a Smile

It costs nothing but creates much.

It enriches those who receive without diminishing the wealth of those who give.

It happens in a flash and the memory of it can last a lifetime.

None are so rich that they can get along without it and none are so poor but are richer for a smile.

It creates happiness in the home, fosters good will in a business and is the countersign of friends.

It is rest to the weary, daylight to the discouraged and nature's best antidote for trouble.

Yet it cannot be bought, begged, or stolen, for it is of no earthly good to anybody until it is given away.

And if some person should be too tired to give you a smile, why not give one of your own?

For nobody needs a smile so much as one who has none to give.

Smile more and watch what happens around you, and within you—whoever and wherever you are.

—Author Unknown

The Way

Every person subscribes to <u>a</u> way of life. What follows is <u>the</u> way as defined in Scripture. "I am the way and the truth and the life." Any way conflicting with this declaration is considered sinful. Sin is destructive. God's way is constructive and spelled out in the Ten Commandments.

The First Commandment:
You shall have no other gods before me.

This means that whatever a person prizes and treasures above everything else is his or her god.

The Second Commandment:
You shall not make for yourself an idol.

This means a person chooses to worship a tangible object (e.g., carved image) rather than the God of the Bible.

The Third Commandment:
You shall not misuse the name of the Lord your God.

This means using God's holy name irreverently and disrespectfully by cursing and asking Him to damn those they dislike.

The Fourth Commandment:
Remember the Sabbath Day by keeping it holy.

This means it is a day of rest and spiritual enhancement. Also, this is a matter of exercising self-discipline. If people aren't content with what they accomplish in six days, chances are they won't be with seven.

The Fifth Commandment:

Honor your father and your mother.

This means children need to be taught to obey and honor their parents. They can't do it on their own. Parents need to be aware that children view them as God. So they need to revere God in their personal lives. The time will come when grown children need not obey them, but they should always honor them.

The Sixth Commandment:

You shall not murder.

This means not killing another person unlawfully. Jesus raised this commandment to a new level when he said, "You shall love your neighbor as yourself." When we fail to do this, we commit emotional murder.

The Seventh Commandment:

You shall not commit adultery.

This means having sex with a person who is not one's spouse. Fornication (premarital sex) is also part of this Commandment because it degrades the uniqueness that each partner brings to the marriage relationship. Promiscuous sex is becoming more prevalent and at a younger age. The thinking is that this is the path to happiness. Little thought is given to the negative consequences, such as unwanted pregnancies, abortions and sexual diseases. Those who choose to ignore the wisdom of responsible sexual conduct conveyed in God's Commandments are in for a rude awakening.

The Eighth Commandment:
You shall not steal.

This means not taking anything that doesn't belong to you. It includes cheating, frauds, false advertising, dishonest work and not treating others the way you want to be treated.

The Ninth Commandment:
You shall not give false testimony against your neighbor.

This means not distorting the truth with intent to deceive.

The Tenth Commandment:
You shall not covet.

This means not to feel extreme envy for possessions or relationships that belong to others. When desire and envy are not kept in check, they become our gods and supersede God of the Bible.

The first four Commandments tell us how to love God, and the remaining six tell us how to love one another. It is all about love. God is love. **The Way** is to love God and love others. God's promise is that those who live lives portrayed by His laws will be blessed and be a blessing to others.

The Way of Love

If I speak in the tongues of men and of angels, but have not love, I am a noisy gong or a clanging cymbal. And if I have prophetic powers, and understand all mysteries and all knowledge, and if I have all faith, so as to remove mountains, but have not love, I am nothing. If I give away all I have, and if I deliver my body to be burned, but have not love, I gain nothing.

Love is patient and kind; love is not jealous or boastful; it is not arrogant or rude. Love does not insist on its own way; it is not irritable or resentful; it does not rejoice at wrong, but rejoices in the right. Love bears all things, believes all things, hopes all things, endures all things.

Love never ends; as for prophecies, they will pass away; as for tongues, they will cease; as for knowledge, it will pass away. For our knowledge is imperfect and our prophecy is imperfect; but when the perfect comes, the imperfect will pass away. When I was a child, I spoke like a child, I reasoned like a child; when I became a man, I gave up childish ways. For now we see in a mirror dimly, but then face to face. Now I know in part; then I shall understand fully, even as I have been fully understood. So faith, hope, love abide, these three; but the greatest of these is love.

—I Corinthians, 13:1-13

The Way of Salvation

Salvation is our greatest need. The Bible teaches that spiritual birth must follow physical birth. "Unless one is born again, he cannot see the kingdom of God." (John 3:3) The choice of spiritual birth is then followed by a gradual growth process that continues throughout life, much like a baby matures to adulthood.

God gives us the only plan for salvation in His Word:

> **Admit** we are sinners: "For all have sinned and fall short of the glory of God." (Romans 3:23) Sin separates us from God. To escape sin's penalty, we need divine forgiveness. It's ours through faith and trust in Jesus.

> **Believe** that Jesus, God in the flesh, died on the cross to pay the penalty for our sins and trust Him for our salvation. "Believe on the Lord Jesus Christ, and you will be saved." (Acts 16:31)

> **Commit** ourselves to obeying God's word. "Therefore, if anyone is in Christ, he is a new creation; old things have passed away; beyond all things have become new." (Corinthians 5:17)

Lord, Jesus, I know I am a sinner and need your forgiveness. I believe you died for my sins. I want to turn from my sins. I now invite you to come into my heart and life. I want to trust and follow you as Lord and Savior. In Thy name I pray. Amen.

The Shape the World Is In

During an interview on national TV several years ago, Billy Graham's daughter was asked, "How could God let something like this [the events of 9-11] happen?" Anne Graham gave an extremely profound and insightful response. She said, "I believe that God is deeply saddened by this, just as we are, but for years we've been telling God to get out of our schools, to get out of our government, and to get out of our lives. And being the gentleman that He is, I believe that He has calmly backed out. How can we expect God to give us His blessing and His protection if we demand that He leave us alone?"

In light of recent events (terrorist attacks, school shootings, etc.), her comments should make us all think. The following statements and scenario of events from the not-so-distant past are worth pondering.

- Madalyn Murray O'Hair (famed atheist) complained she didn't want any prayer in our schools. We said OK. (She was found murdered.)

- Someone said you better not read the Bible in school. (The Bible says that you should not kill or steal and that you should love your neighbor as yourself.) We said OK.

- Dr. Benjamin Spock said we shouldn't spank our children when they misbehave because their little personalities would be warped and we might damage their self esteem. We said an expert should know what he's talking about, so we said OK. (Dr. Spock's own son committed suicide.)

- Someone said teachers and principals should not discipline our children when they misbehave. The school administrators said no faculty member in their school should touch a student when they misbehave because they didn't want any bad publicity, and they surely didn't want to be sued. (There is a big difference between disciplining and touching, beating, smacking, humiliating, kicking, etc.) We said OK.

- Someone said to let our daughters have abortions if they want, and they won't even have to tell their parents. We said OK.

- A school board member said that since "boys will be boys" and they are going to do it anyway, let's give our sons all the condoms they want, so they can have all the fun they desire, and we won't have to tell their parents they got them at school. We said OK.

- Some of our top elected officials said it doesn't matter what we do in private as long as we do our jobs. Agreeing with them, we said it doesn't matter what anyone, including the President, does in private, as long as we have a job and the economy is good.

- Someone said to print magazines with pictures of nude women and call it wholesome, down-to-earth appreciation for the beauty of the female body. We said OK.

- Someone else took that appreciation a step further and published pictures of nude children and then stepped further still by making them available on the Internet; after all, they are entitled to free speech. We said OK.

- The entertainment industry said, "Let's make TV shows and movies that promote profanity, violence, and illicit sex. Let's record music that encourages rape, drugs, murder, suicide, and satanic themes." We said that it was just entertainment and it has no adverse effect. Nobody takes it seriously any-way, so go right ahead.

- The lewd, crude, vulgar and obscene passes freely through cyberspace, but the public discussion of God is suppressed in the school and the workplace.

- "Dear God, why didn't you save the little girl killed in her classroom? Sincerely, Concerned Student." The reply: "Dear Concerned Student, I am not allowed in schools. Sincerely, God."

- How simple it is for people to trash God and then wonder why the world is going to hell. Why do we believe what the newspapers say, but question what the Bible says? How can someone say, "I believe in God," but then still follow Satan who, by the way, also "believes" in God?

- How can someone be so fired up for Christ on Sunday, but be an invisible Christian the rest of the week? People are more worried about what other people think of us than what God thinks of us.

Now we are asking ourselves why our children have no con-science, why they don't know right from wrong, and why it doesn't bother them to kill strangers, their classmates and themselves. If only we would take the time to really think about it, we might improve ourselves, and our behavior would be an example to others. If not, then we have no one to blame but ourselves when we sit back and complain about what bad shape the world is in! **We reap what we sow.**

Time

Time is something in very limited supply. Why not invest it in our children? When parents spend time with their children, they pay them the highest compliment they will ever receive. The Bible cautions us about not taking time for granted. "Whereas, you do not know what will happen tomorrow. For what is your life? It is even a vapor that appears for a little time and then vanishes away."

Using time wisely means establishing priorities. Children should be first on your list. They can't wait. You should be involved with every facet of their lives. Children can't survive physically or emotionally when left on their own. They need loving care and guidance especially during the pre-school years. This is when they can best absorb the character-building values they will need the rest of their lives. "Train up a child in the way he should go, and when he is old he will not depart from it." If these values are not learned at an early age, they may never be learned. The Bible tells us: "To everything there is a season, a time for every purpose under heaven. A time to be born, and a time to die; a time to plant and a time to pluck what is planted."

Time between parents and children is needed to focus on the following:

1. Enjoying them for what they are.

2. Building up their self-esteem.

3. Helping them set small and large goals.

4. Making home a happy place to be.

5. Teaching them to accept the bad along with the good.

6. Helping them to be good at as many things as possible.

7. Encouraging them to become as independent as possible.

8. Helping them develop realistic self-concepts.

9. Showing them how to do things.

10. Reading to them.

11. Loving, talking, singing, touching and playing.

12. Allowing them to help.

13. Getting to know each other.

14. Learning about God and praying together.

15. Encouraging them to make the most of their God-given gifts.

16. Acknowledging differences in children by not comparing them.

Time spent with children helps parents learn about their personalities, opinions and talents. What a joy to discover the individual God created! Time with your children is a priceless gift from God. Wasting time dishonors Him.

Truth

What is truth? Webster defines truth as the quality or fact of being true, honest, sincere, accurate, etc. More specifically, it is in agreement with an established standard or rule. For example, if you ask three different people what the temperature is, you will get three different answers. But if you want the truth, check the thermometer yourself.

There are all kinds of truth out there. As someone so aptly put it: "There are three truths: my truth, your truth and THE truth." The definition of truth as used here is God's word, the Bible—the pillar and foundation of belief in absolute truth, where hundreds of references speak words of truth always in love.

Godly truth is determined by God's word (God-centered), the Ten Commandments in particular. Worldly truth (self-centered) is determined by the culture. All truth is relevant; Bible truth never changes—it is the same "yesterday and today and forever." Worldly truth is the opposite; it is in constant change. Nothing is absolute—anything goes. Whenever these differences are ignored, negative consequences are sure to follow.

"The Parable of the Sower" is a short, simple, worldly story that teaches Godly truth. Jesus said, "A farmer went out to sow his seed. As he was scattering the seed, some fell along the path; it was trampled on, and the birds of the air ate it up. Some fell on rock, and when it came up, the plants withered because they had no moisture. Other seed fell among thorns, which grew up with it and choked the plants. Still other seed fell on good soil. It came up and yielded a crop a hundred times more than was sown."

Jesus' disciples asked him what this parable meant. "This is the meaning of the parable: Those along the path are the ones who hear, and then the devil comes and takes away the word from their hearts, so that they may not believe and be saved. Those on the rock are the ones who receive the word with joy when they hear it, but they have no root. They believe for a while, but in the time of testing they fall away. The seed that fell among thorns stands for those who hear, but as they go on their way they are choked by life's worries, riches and pleasures, and they do not mature. But the seed on good soil stands for those with a noble and good heart, who hear the word, retain it, and by persevering produce a crop." Which soil best describes you? Does this parable imply that only one out of four people can be counted on to tell the truth and abide in God's word?

The 9th Commandment says, "You shall not give false testimony." Do not be disloyal toward others by withholding or distorting the truth with intent to deceive. Remember, God loves every person equally. In the words of J. Grant Howard, "Truth is not limited *to* the Scriptures, but it is limited *by* the Scriptures."

When it comes to what is really true, we must admit that certain truths never change. If it is true, it's true, whether people believe it or not. Truths are timeless. They provide guidance when making tough decisions. They add meaning and give purpose to life. They have served us well in the past. The more people stray from Biblical principles, the more disheartening the present and future will become.

Now we are beginning to ask ourselves why our children have no conscience, why they don't know right from wrong; and why it doesn't bother them to kill strangers, their classmates and themselves. If only we would take the time to really think about it, we might improve ourselves, and our behavior would be an example to others. If not, then we have no one to blame but ourselves when we sit back and complain about what bad shape the world is in. We reap what we sow.

"To love our neighbor as ourselves is such a truth for regulating human society, that by that alone one might determine all the cases in social morality."—John Locke

Waste

Waste has become one of the most critical issues in our present-day culture. It's a matter of using or spending without real need or purpose and without restraint, good sense and consideration for others.

Waste is much more than filling up our trash cans. It's the inconsiderate and unnecessary use of time, money, water, energy, unhealthy food, effort, talent or any other valuable resource. It's what is squandered after are needs are met. It's carelessness; it's thoughtlessness; it's irresponsible behavior.

We can't do wrong and have it turn out right; someone, somewhere, someplace, will experience the negative consequences of our irresponsible actions. For example, utility experts say that we waste as much energy as we really need because lights, appliances and water are often left on when not needed. These are just a few ways of preventing waste.

When all is said and done, minimizing waste comes down to dollars and "sense." Adults, and especially those who are parents, need to teach their children the value of money as early as possible. Children must limit their spending within the amount allotted them or even save some for something that might crop up in the future. If they mismanage their allowance, they must live with their mistakes—the price of learning the value of money. Debt, spending money one does not have, should be avoided by all at all cost.

Waste by a single individual may appear as very insignificant, but when millions and millions of people are involved the additional expenses and the additional resources required can be overwhelming. At one time waste was actually viewed as sin because all stand to suffer as a result of it. Just as wasteful actions produce negative consequences, the opposite is just as true: actions that prevent waste can generate positive results. Thus, all can reap the benefits. All need to learn to think about the welfare of others and not just their own.

People must learn to distinguish between needs and wants. The Lord's prayer teaches, "Give us this day our daily bread [needs]," not our daily wants; there's a big difference between the two. A few principles to help reduce waste include the following: *use it up, make it do, wear it out* and *do without*.

It's never too early to exercise giving to charity and savings. As children grow older, encourage them to get a part-time job and open a savings account. As difficult as it may seem at times, the more parents persist, the more likely children will avoid waste and establish wise savings and spending habits that will last them a lifetime.

Ways to Simplify Your Life

Nearly half of Americans feel they don't have enough time. Yet there are those who have discovered that the gift of life is realized one brief moment at a time. It's time to slow down and start savoring life—it's not as hard as you think.

It's time to simplify. That means being aware of how you spend your money, time and energy. Here are 10 easy steps to get you started in simplifying your life and finding precious time.

Start the day right. Save all the frantic wasted time used in the morning to prepare for the day. Spend the night before preparing for the next day.

Declutter your space. It takes energy to keep possessions in working order or dusted. Get rid of stuff that's broken or missing a part.

Learn to say "no." Don't overload your schedule with more tasks, more jobs, and more volunteer time. It's OK to say no.

Turn off the TV. We waste too much time sitting in front of the TV. Curb how many hours the TV is on. And before you pick up the remote control, ask yourself if there are activities to share with the family, like a museum or a play, that you've been putting off.

Commit to No. 1. When the demands of work, parenthood, or housework chores get you down, it's time to schedule a date with yourself. Whether it's every Sunday night or 20 minutes each morning, the important thing is to make a plan and stick to it.

Find a sanctuary. Escape to a place to enjoy peaceful solitude.

Be spontaneous. Spontaneity is key to feeling like you're in control of your own destiny. Every once in a while, a change in routine can spark your spirits and your energy.

Live beneath your means. Did you know that eighty percent of American's self-made millionaires are frugal? If you want to achieve economic independence, try buying only what you can afford, not what you think you need. See how long you can go without cashing a check, charging on credit or buying anything.

Rewrite the course of your day. When the newspaper's horoscope doesn't tell you what you want to hear, write your own, using words that make you feel great. Or start jotting down phrases you like on slips of paper, put them in a box, and pack as many as you need to start the day.

Listen to your body. You know what your biological clock prefers. Indulge it and watch your productivity grow.

— "Life Savors: How to Simplify Your Life"
Ohio State University Extension

What's Right? What's Wrong?

No two words in any language provoke more controversy than **right** and **wrong.** Although there are exceptions, most people agree that a universal code of ethics does exist. Any kind of order would be impossible unless all civilized people have a set of principles that determine responsible behavior. C. S. Lewis wrote, "We know that people find themselves under a moral law, which they did not make and cannot quite forget even when they try, and which they know they ought to obey."

Most agree that no society could survive without moral laws that spell out right and wrong conduct. The question then becomes: Whose morality will be legislated? All laws intrude on the morality of someone. Are there moral principles and guidelines that have withstood the unfailing test of time? I believe the answer is yes!

In our culture, we often discover too late that what we thought was right turns out to be wrong and what we thought was wrong turns out to be right. This essay speaks to right and wrong – responsible conduct for all: those with religious affiliation to atheists and everyone in between.

Consider the following sample selection of right moral values and guiding principles: fairness, honesty, justice, kindness, loyalty, love, respect; their opposites constitute wrong. Right moral choices produce positive results and wrong moral choices produce negative results.

There is a powerful force at work in our lives; it is referred to as sin. Sin (vice) is any action that is detrimental to oneself or others. Traditionally, the seven most serious and deadly sins are anger or rage, greed, envy, gluttony, pride, lust and laziness. When choosing sin (and there are many others than these seven) over what's right, the consequences can be so very destructive. It is real and its power to condemn is deadly. Many rationalize that some actions are not sinful—after all, "everybody does it." With most people, when they do wrong, it isn't because they don't know what's right; in fact, the opposite is true. They do everything possible to conceal what they have done, hoping no one will know. This is like taking poison when nobody is looking; it still will kill you. Sin destroys!

In the words of Gregory Koull, "If you believe that morality is a matter of personal definition, then you surrender the possibility of making any moral judgments on anyone else's actions ever again, no matter how offensive to your intuitive sense of right or wrong."

Our self-centeredness tells us it is not wrong to do what we think is right, even if others suffer from it. For wrong to turn out right negates the fact that we reap what we sow. These individuals are not discouraged from doing wrong because they fail to acknowledge that, down the road of life, they will suffer the consequences of their inappropriate conduct. It behooves people to avoid doing wrong if for no other reason than the results will be to their advantage rather than their disadvantage.

When it comes to what is truly important, we must admit that certain RIGHTS and WRONGS never change. They are timeless truths that provide guidance when facing tough issues. They worked in the past; they work in the present; they will continue to be true and work in the future. Each person is responsible for deciding which path to take and what choices to make.

So, how does one really know what's right or what's wrong? The answer is simple: Look inward; judge only yourself; do to others what you would like done to you or, perhaps, your children.

What to Say
When We Pass Away

I'M FREE

Don't grieve for me, for now I'm free.
I'm following that path God laid for me.

I took his hand when I heard him call.
I turned my back and left it all.

I could not stay another day
To laugh, to love, to work or play.

Tasks left undone must stay that way.
I found that peace at close of day.

If my parting has left a void,
then fill it with remembered joy.

A friendship shared, a laugh, a kiss,
as yes, these things I too will miss.

Be not burdened with times of sorrow.
I wish you the sunshine of tomorrow.

My life's been full; I've savored much:
good friends, good times, a loved one's touch.

Perhaps my time seemed all too brief.
Don't lengthen it now with undue grief.

Lift up your hearts and share with me.
God wanted me now; He set me free.

—Author Unknown

MISS ME—BUT LET ME GO

When I come to the end of the road, and the sun has set for me,
I want no rites in a gloom-filled room. Why cry for a soul set free?

Miss me a little—but not too long and not with your head bowed low.
Remember the love that we once shared. Miss me—but let me go.

For this is a journey that we all must take, and each must go alone.
It's all part of the Master's plan, a step on the road to home.

When you are lonely and sick at heart, go to the friends we know.
And bury your sorrows in doing good deeds. Miss me—but let me go.

—Author Unknown

Which One Are You?

The winner is always a part of the answer; the loser is always a part of the problem.

The winner says, "Let me do it for you"; the loser says, "That's not my job."

The winner sees an answer for every problem; the loser sees a problem in every answer.

The winner sees a green near every sand trap; the loser sees two or three sand traps near every green.

The winner says, "It may be difficult but it's possible"; the loser says, "It may be possible but it's too difficult.

You can't "win 'em all," but you can choose to be a winner rather than a loser. A winner accepts defeat, gets up, and goes on.

The difference is attitude. And we're not stuck with our attitudes. We learned them; we can "unlearn" them. "It may be difficult, but it's possible."

— *Executive Digest*

Winners and Losers

Who is a winner? Who is a loser? By definition, winners advance in life and movement is in a positive direction. They are viewed as conquerors, gainers and victorious. Losers regress in life and movement is in a negative direction. They are viewed as defeated, hopeless and overcome. What follows is my attempt to answer these questions.

Most people subscribe to one of two ways of living: God-centered, following spiritual and moral laws shielding us from much of life's needless suffering, which better allows us to live more meaningful lives (winners); world-centered, following cultural patterns and values, which have been popular in the past, many remaining so in the present, and new and different ones appearing in the future (losers). Godly principles remain the same; worldly standards tend to constantly change over the years. "The wisdom of this world is foolishness in God's sight." (1 Corinthians 3:19)

Character traits distinguish one person from another. People with good character traits are accountable, caring, fair, honest, kind, loving, sincere, trustworthy and more—winners. If practicing these principles produces positive results, then the consequences of doing the opposite most assuredly will be negative—losers.

Two examples of character traits that support these positions are humility and vanity. Humility is God-centered. "It's not all about me." The humble person acknowledges his or her own weaknesses and faults and then seeks wise counsel to correct them. The humble person is calm, giving, modest, obedient and more—a winner.

Vanity is self-centered. "It's all about me." The vain person focuses on "getting," and tends to be arrogant, conceited, egotistical, smug and more—a loser. "Good people do the good things that are in them. But evil people do the evil things that are in them." (Matthew 12:35)

179

Our attitude dictates our behavior. No matter what the facts or circumstances, we have the power to choose how we view them, negatively or positively. Our attitude is the only thing over which we have any control. To assign blame only prevents us from dealing with any given situation. The winner says, "It may be difficult, but it's possible"; the loser says, "It may be possible, but it's too difficult." Our actions determine the consequences.

So, what are *you*? What would you like to be? Life is all about choices. Remember that God is love and we are all equally loved. Live your life loving and "lifting" others and you will lift yourself—a guaranteed winner!

Why We Are the Way We Are

What makes us the way we are? First, our heredity: the passing on of certain characteristics from parents to offspring—the genes we inherit at conception. Second, our environment: all the things, conditions and influences that surround us, both positive and negative, especially during the early, pre-school years. Third, prenatal health care.

In *Origins: How the Nine Months Before Birth Shape the Rest of Our Lives,* author Annie Murphy Paul writes the following: "Much of what a pregnant woman encounters in her daily life—the air she breathes, the food and drink she consumes, the chemicals she's exposed to, even the emotions she feels—is shared in some fashion with her fetus." She continues, noting that these factors shape a person as a baby and a child and continue to have an effect throughout life.

Children respond to their environment based to a great extent on their inherited characteristics. However, they should not be made to feel inferior or cheated because of hereditary differences. They have no control over it. They can't change it. And their worth as a human being should not depend on it. It's God's plan for them to be different. Therefore, they should not be compared to one another. When parents view their children in this light, they not only prevent them from feeling inferior or superior, but also they actually help them discover God's plan for their lives.

> "One of the most important gifts a parent can give a child is the gift of that child's uniqueness. Children's parents are the very best people to let them know that they are different, that there are no others in the whole world who are exactly like them, and that their differences are part of what makes them special and lovable.

When parents value their child's uniqueness, that child can learn self-worth and the worth of others as well."

—Fred Rogers

Since heredity is pre-determined there's little parents can do about it. But, they can do a lot about environment and this can make the biggest difference in how children turn out. One of the most critical factors in children's lives is their environment. At the moment of conception environment impacts on children physically, emotionally and mentally. It's up to parents to provide a good environment for their children. A healthy environment would include such things as providing safe conditions in which to grow up; adapting discipline to the individual child; spending as much time as possible with them; correcting them in a loving way; focusing on their strengths; instilling a positive attitude, "catching" them doing right; helping them acquire a healthy self-image; making children feel special; and supplying healthy physical and spiritual food.

Everything children experience in the environment is recorded in their minds—forever! The more positive and caring the environment is, the better children will respond and thrive.

Children's minds at birth are like newly plowed fields. What grows will be determined by the quality of the soil, the kind of seeds planted and the care given. These factors will determine the quality and quantity of fruit produced. Something is going to grow, if not the preferred seeds, then weeds. Once the seeds are planted, the kind of fruit probably won't change.

We are the way we are primarily because of our heredity, environment and prenatal health. These are far from exhaustive and the reader is encouraged to find and take advantage of whatever measures that would enhance self, other family members and others with whom one comes in contact. Over a lifetime, we reap what we sow!

Worry

Parents should encourage children to trust God in all things. "Trust in the Lord with all your heart, and lean not on your own understanding." This kind of wisdom takes the worry out of living. Throughout life children will encounter situations they can do nothing about. These must be accepted as part of God's divine plan. They need focus on those situations they can do something about. Children have to move in the direction of taking on more and more responsibility for their actions. God has given them a mind and He expects them to use it. Children need to learn to take charge of their lives and not have it the other way around.

Parents should help their children avoid the worry habit. It's acquired. We aren't born with it. It's destructive. Doctors tell us that worry by far is the greatest cause of illness. Symptoms of excessive worry in children include nail biting, hair pulling, overeating, digestive problems, elimination difficulties, depression and many more. Not only does worry hurt children emotionally and physically, but also it undermines their faith and trust in God which compounds the problem even more.

God doesn't want anybody to be a slave to worry. "Be anxious for nothing, but in everything by prayer and supplication, with thanksgiving, let your requests be made known to God, and the peace of God which surpasses all understanding, will guard your hearts and minds through Christ Jesus." When children come to the understanding that everything that worries them can be placed under God's control, then His word will lead them to peace, joy and confidence.

Parents have to help children sort through the things they worry about. This means separating those things they can do something about from those they can't. They will soon learn that most things people worry about never happen. And those that do aren't nearly as bad as imagined. This will allow them to focus on the present and deal with matters that require their attention. "This is the day the Lord has made; we will rejoice and be glad in it."

Worriers can become so occupied with the past and future that the present gets ignored. Living is not unlike driving a car. Occasionally, drivers should look back and far ahead. But mostly they should look at the road immediately in front of them. When children learn from yesterday and concentrate on today, tomorrow usually takes care of itself.

Children worry most when they experience fear and anxiety that their needs will not be met. Simply telling them not to worry doesn't get the job done. Little children are totally dependent on their parents. They trust them and expect them to be wise in looking out for their welfare. Children need such things as the following: Good physical and spiritual food; warm and tender care; unconditional love; protection and security; help in succeeding; a positive attitude; freedom from comparison; acceptance; recognition; discipline; praise; encouragement; compliments; and appreciation.

When children's needs are met, worry will have a hard time taking root.

Yesterday—Today—Tomorrow

There are two days in every week about which we should not worry, two days that should be kept free from fear and apprehension.

One of these days is **Yesterday** with its mistakes and cares, its faults and blunders, its aches and pains. **Yesterday** has passed forever beyond our control.

All the money in the world cannot bring back **Yesterday**. We cannot undo a single act we performed; we cannot erase a single word we said—**Yesterday** is gone.

The other day we should not worry about is **Tomorrow** with its possible adversities, its burdens, its large promise and poor performance. **Tomorrow** is also beyond our immediate control.

Tomorrow's sun will rise, either in splendor or beyond a mask of clouds — but it will rise. Until it does, we have no stake in **Tomorrow**, for it is as yet unborn.

This leaves only one day—**Today**. Anyone can fight the battle of just one day. It is only when you and I add the burden of those two awful eternities—**Yesterday** and **Tomorrow**—that we break down.

It is not the experience of **Today** that drives us mad; it is the remorse or bitterness for something that has happened **Yesterday** and the dread of what **Tomorrow** may bring.

Let us, therefore, live **Today**.

—Author Unknown

Let us hear the conclusion of the whole matter: Fear [revere] God, and keep his commandments: for this is the whole duty of man. For God shall bring every work into judgment, with every secret thing, whether it is good or evil.

—Ecclesiastes 12:13-14

CPSIA information can be obtained
at www.ICGtesting.com
Printed in the USA
FFOW05n0206100314

9 781604 147599